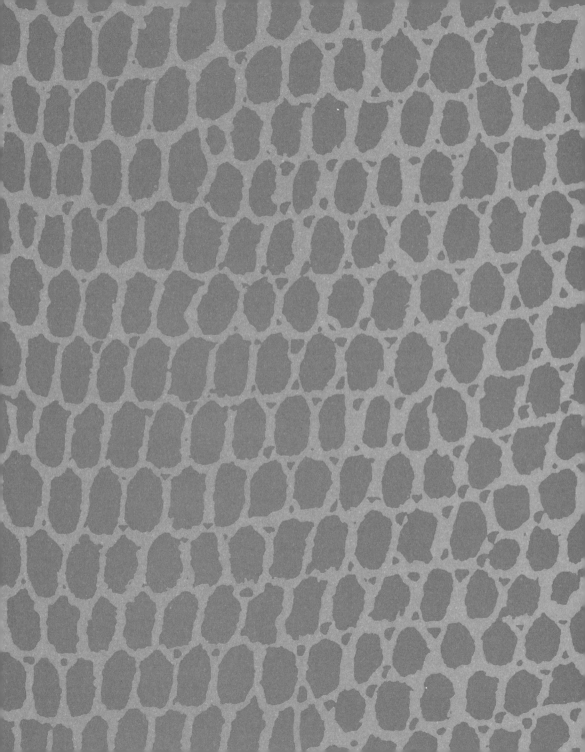

Animal Planet™

Aquarium Care of Fancy Guppies

STAN SHUBEL

ANIMAL PLANET ∨ PET CARE LIBRARY

Aquarium Care of Fancy Guppies

Project Team
Editor: Brian Scott
Copy Editor: Mary Connell
Interior Design: Leah Lococo Ltd. and Stephanie Krautheim
Design Layout: Angela Stanford

T.F.H. Publications
President/CEO: Glen S. Axelrod
Executive Vice President: Mark E. Johnson
Publisher: Christopher T. Reggio
Production Manager: Kathy Bontz

T.F.H. Publications, Inc.
One TFH Plaza
Third and Union Avenues
Neptune City, NJ 07753

Discovery Communications, Inc.
  Book Development Team
Maureen Smith, Executive Vice President & General
  Manager, Animal Planet
Carol LeBlanc, Vice President, Marketing and Retail
  Development
Elizabeth Bakacs, Vice President, Creative Services
Peggy Ang, Director, Animal Planet Marketing
Caitlin Erb, Marketing Associate

 Exterior design ©2006 Discovery Communications, Inc. Animal Planet, logo and Animusings are trademarks of Discovery Communications, Inc., used under license. All rights reserved. animalplanet.com

Interior design, text, and photos ©2006 T.F.H. Publications, Inc.

Printed and bound in China.
06 07 08 09 10 1 3 5 7 9 8 6 4 2

Shubel, Stan.
  Aquarium care of guppies / Stan Shubel.
    p. cm.
  Includes bibliographical references and index.
  ISBN 0-7938-3764-2 (alk. paper)
  1. Guppies. I. Title.
  SF458.G8S58 2006
  639.3'7667–dc22
  2006013111

This book has been published with the intent to provide accurate and authoritative information in regard to the subject matter within. While every precaution has been taken in preparation of this book, the author and publisher expressly disclaim responsibility for any errors, omissions, or adverse effects arising from the use or application of the information contained herein. The techniques and suggestions are used at the reader's discretion and are not to be considered a substitute for veterinary care. If you suspect a medical problem consult your veterinarian.

The Leader in Responsible Animal Care for Over 50 Years!™

www.tfhpublications.com

CENTRAL
Garden & Pet

Table of Contents

Introduction

The guppy, or *Poecilia reticulata* as this fish species is known scientifically, has been available, in various forms, to the aquarium hobby for more than one hundred years. They are collected from various locations in South America and the islands of Barbados and Trinidad. However, the wild guppy brought to America and Europe from its native lands bears little resemblance to the fish we see in pet shops and fish shows today.

Chapter 1

Why do YOU Want to

Keep Guppies?

Guppies are magnificent little fish and there are many reasons why you might want to keep them, or why you're already keeping them. Their color, their behavior, their personality, and many other factors all contribute to the huge popularity and demand that guppies bring to the aquarium world. Few, if any, other fishes are kept and bred in the quantities that guppies are, and the number of strains available to guppy fanciers today is absolutely huge.

Throughout this book, you'll not only have access to some of the best information available on breeding and raising guppies, but you'll also be exposed to tips and techniques. Ideas in this book will hopefully inspire young people to be better caretakers of nature's offspring, which in this case is the beloved fancy guppy.

Guppies in Nature

The guppy *(Poecilia reticulata)* is found in the wild throughout extreme northern South America and adjacent islands including, but not limited to, Trinidad, the Netherlands Antilles, the Windward Islands, Barbados, Grenada, the Leeward Islands, Saint Thomas, and Antigua.

The Expert Knows

Perfect Guppy Tanks

The perfect guppy aquarium is one that is low and wide. Filtration should be steady but not too strong. The water temperature should be maintained around 76°F (24°C), with pH around 7.0 and moderate hardness. Partial water changes should be done frequently and at a volume of no less than one third the total volume of the tank at each change. Water changes are key to a healthy aquarium and success with guppies.

Fancy Guppy Origins

In aquariums, the various wild populations have been extensively crossed with one another. This random hybridization and subsequent selective breeding gave rise to today's highly cultivated fancy guppy forms.

Venezuela and Guyana have the highest natural densities of these fish on mainland South America. They can also be found in isolated areas as far north as Southern Mexico.

Fin coloration varies according to population. In many regions, aquarium and pond-bred fish are exposed to open air and thus they naturally take part in mosquito control measures to some degree; feeding on these natural pests affect the finnage and coloration of these fish.

Genuine populations of guppies in the wild are much more consistent in coloration than many hobbyists who are familiar only with the cultivated forms might suspect. Females are variable in base color, having a gray, greenish-gray, brown, or olive-brown coloring with grayish-white belly and

Fancy Guppy Origins

In aquariums, the various wild populations have been extensively crossed with one another. This random hybridization and subsequent selective breeding gave rise to today's highly cultivated fancy guppy forms.

basically colorless fins. Males have a dotted pattern involving green, blue, black, red, and yellow depending upon the population. The Peacock's eye design is typical of that found in wild populations, too. This "eye" consists of a colored center surrounded by a pigmented ring often located on the upper part of the caudal peduncle. The dorsal fin is only slightly drawn out into a pennant. The caudal fin is usually rounded but may show a little bit of a sword at the upper part (Wischnath, 1993).

Relaxation & Fascination

A tank filled with fancy-tailed guppies is one of the most beautiful, and relaxing, sights to behold in the aquarium world. Many times, hobbyists who wish to keep guppies of various strains and who are not worried about whether they will hybridize, will put together fantastically beautiful displays of colored guppies of all types.

In addition to the relaxing effect a tank of guppies provides, these fish are also just plain fascinating to watch. Their inquisitive behavior and the males' way of relentlessly chasing after the females and sparring with opposing males is, quite intriguing. Children, especially, get a kick out of guppys' antics and when they are put in charge of their own guppy tank, they learn a lot about responsibility and caring for the well-being of other living creatures.

Endler's Livebearers (Poecilia wingei) *were once considered the same species as guppies (*P. reticulata) *but have now been given their own species status.*

Guppies are beautiful little fishes that brighten up any aquarium they swim in.

A Slice of Nature

Recently, there has been an increase in the interest in aquariums, simply because people feel a close connection with nature when an aquarium is present in their home or office. Without a doubt, a miniature recapturing of the natural beauty of a mountain creek or lowlands pool is a wonderful thing—of course it is! And to actually be able to care for such a unique, albeit man-made slice of nature is nothing short of impressive.

Since guppies are small fish, they only need a small tank, say under 10 gallons (38 l). This allows hobbyists to set up and effectively maintain an aquarium—or series of aquariums—to replicate a slice of nature in their home or office. Guppy display tanks are quite impressive to say the least, and best of all—it's easily possible for you to set one up!

While the caring for any pet has proven to reduce stress and decrease hypertension, aquariums are particularly effective at achieving this result. In fact, many doctor's and dentist's offices have at least one

SMALL FRY

Guppy Love

Guppies are easy to fall in love with. Their charming antics and cheery behavior are an instant attraction to hobbyists—especially young hobbyists.

Aquarium Watching is Good for You!

Unfortunately, stress is a part of our lives but how we manage stress is just as important as how we try to prevent it. Finding various relaxation techniques is one way to help alleviate stress build-up and very few techniques work better than sitting in front of a large aquarium and watching the fish swim by.

aquarium situated in the waiting room for patients to observe before they meet with the caregiver.

Studies have shown that displaying aquariums of brightly colored fishes actually curtailed the often disruptive behaviors of Alzheimer patients

and increased their desire to eat as well. Other studies have proven that aquariums can actually have a calming effect upon children who are diagnosed with attention deficit/hyperactivity disorder (ADHD).

Guppy Behavior

Guppies are unique little fish in that they are very peaceful, so much so in fact that you simply cannot keep them with many other types of fishes. While more on this subject will be covered later in this book, it's important to mention it here, too. Guppies, and especially fancy strains of guppies, are often targets of aggression from tankmates of other species. Even relatively peaceful tankmates will often become uncharacteristically aggressive when guppies are around.

A few guppies in an aquarium make for an excellent stress reliever.

Chapter 2

Getting Started & Keeping It

Running

Guppies are often kept or bred in sterile, unfurnished aquariums. This is the preferred technique of professional guppy breeders whose focus is not "aquarium beautiful;" they are concentrating instead on the fish themselves and their bloodlines. The professional breeder constantly tends to his or her fish and supervises their condition, and such supervision, combined with regular water changes, allows the guppies to achieve their maximum potential in growth and beauty.

Guppies will do well in a community setting as long as their tankmates don't nip at their fins.

Casual hobbyists are not expected to take such stringent care of their fish but are expected to keep them healthy and thriving. A bare aquarium is not needed for this, as guppies do quite well in a peaceful community set-ting.

Aquarium Selection

Whether you are shooting for a decorator-look aquarium or banks of aquariums with generations of high-quality broodstock, you are going to need a vessel that reliably contains the water so necessary for their lives.

Glass Aquariums

All-glass aquariums are the most practical ones to use—they are the most commonly used type of aquarium worldwide. Small to medium-sized glass aquariums are not heavy and most folks are able to move them with ease, albeit carefully. Additionally, they are moderately priced, a far cheaper alternative compared to other types of aquariums. Take care, however, to see that they are resting on a level surface. Yet another advantage is that you can drain them and keep them dry for extended periods of time without fearing that they will leak when you refill them.

Acrylic Aquariums

Acrylic aquariums are gaining market share, and well they should. They are very light and easy to move. Acrylic tanks are available in some interesting shapes for those of us who want a real showcase for some prize guppies in a beautifully decorated aquarium. On the downside, however, hobbyists have to be very careful not to scratch acrylic aquariums during cleaning and general maintenance.

Bowls

The one-gallon (3.8 l) drum bowl is an indispensable piece of equipment with a number of uses for the guppy hobbyist and breeder. Drum bowls will hold baby fish until you have a tank ready for them. They are handy for getting a good look at potential breeders, for separating females ready to drop their young, or even for isolating sick fish.

From a practical standpoint, it is much easier to medicate a small bowl of water to treat a diseased fish than a whole tank—especially since so many medications will destroy the bacterial balance in the aquarium.

Rack Setups

Since many guppy hobbyists tend to have more than one aquarium devoted to various fishes, it's only fitting to include rack setups here as well. Rack setups, or simply racks, are used to house several aquariums all on one common base. This allows the tanks to be serviced easily and more conveniently than those spread all over one's house.

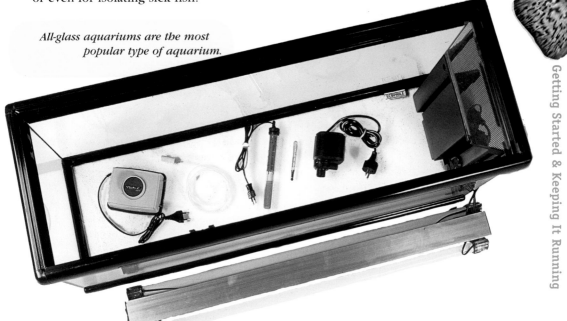

All-glass aquariums are the most popular type of aquarium.

The author's fishroom consists of multiple rack setups.

When planning your rack setup, try to figure out how many tanks you will be placing on it. Are they going to be placed lengthwise or endwise, and how many rows of them will there be? Of course, always be sure to leave enough room to allow you to work on the tanks in between the levels easily.

A common rack setup consists of three levels, with the top row at eye level and the bottom row at about knee level. Many hobbyists don't really like to have the bottom level that low but it makes it easier to fit a large number of tanks in a small area. Just below the mid-level row, you can run PVC pipe the length of the row with an inverted opening every few feet for draining the tanks without having to

carry buckets of water. In some setups, this drain pipe might be below the bottom level of aquariums. But, more than likely you'll be doing something like this in a basement and therefore need to pump the water up and into a sewer or your septic system. So, you may have to have a collection basin where a low drain pipe may normally be utilized. Or a self-priming pump can be used to siphon water from the tanks into the drain.

The racks themselves are most commonly made of wood, like 2 x 4s or something of that nature. Be sure to use a good grade of lumber, primed and painted, in order to resist water damage. If you do build your own racks, make sure that you have enough

supports so the rails don't sag at all. Some breeders use angle-iron racks and others have developed their own custom designs. It's really all just a matter of personal preference and how much you really want to spend.

Show Tanks

An attractively planted aquarium with a school of perky, healthy guppies and even other species of compatible fishes is not difficult to set up and maintain. On the contrary, if you are primarily interested in keeping guppies rather than breeding them, it is best to maintain them in a fully furnished, beautifully decorated aquarium. You will soon see that a decorated guppy show tank is just a little more work and certainly much more pleasing to the eye than a sterile breeding tank is any day. It is this pleasure that helps to ensure that the guppies get the attention they need from busy hobbyists.

Breeding Tanks

If, however, you are very serious about breeding high-quality show guppies, there are certain things you must do. Depending on how many lines, or strains, you intend to raise, you'll need a minimum of six aquariums for each line. The best tanks are small ones, in the 5- to 10-gallon (19 to 38 l) range, for breeding the parents and raising the young. For older, larger

Small aquariums of 5 to 10 gallon capacity make the best breeding tanks.

guppies, a 15-gallon (56 l) tank may be required. Over the years, various aquariums have been tried and tested but the 10-gallon (38 l) tank has always been a favorite among professionals. You may find that you can raise guppies in even larger aquariums and that's fine, experiment to find out which size tank will work best for you. However, a point to consider is that smaller tanks are far easier to handle when it comes time to clean and move them. Once you've wrestled with a 50-gallon (189 l) aquarium and tried to place it back on its stand after cleaning it, you'll come to appreciate the smaller sizes.

Aquarium Placement & Stand Selection

With a weight of 8.3 pounds (3.7 kg) per gallon, even the smallest aquarium is generally considered to be quite heavy. To provide the support that your aquarium needs, you will need to have a stand that will hold its weight. In turn, aquarium stands themselves can be quite heavy, which will, of course, add to the overall weight and pressure being exerted on your floor.

Tank Placement

Before you read any further information, take a look at the location where you're considering placing your tank setup. It is surprisingly common for someone to assemble everything for their new aquarium, and only after it is placed and filled with water, do they discover there isn't any outlet nearby to provide electricity for the tank's equipment. So, make sure your location has direct access to electricity. Next, make sure there is no direct rays of sunlight that would come in and shine on the tank. You don't want sunlight for any amount of time, not even an hour or more.

Once you have chosen a spot that has electricity but no direct sunlight, you are ready to check the most important thing of all—the floor! Your floor should be solid. If you are fortunate enough to have a concrete slab under the chosen area—great; if not, make sure the floor is able to

Weighty Matters

Don't underestimate the weight of an aquarium! Figure on approximately 10 pounds for every gallon. This takes into account the weight of the tank, gravel, and water. A 55-gallon tank, therefore, weighs in at about a quarter ton!

hold the combined weight of the aquarium setup. Remember that the tank, with all of its equipment, is going to be far heavier than what most people can readily pick up by themselves. Add water and you have yourself a seriously heavy piece of furniture.

Proper Support

A solid floor may be first in importance with regard to supporting your aquarium, but a solid stand is definitely a close second. If you build your own wooden stand or rack, you can customize it to fit whatever size tanks you wish to use. In addition, many manufacturers offer warranties

Be sure to check, and double check, the level of your aquarium before filling it.

if you buy a combined aquarium and a stand from them. This is by far the most highly recommended route to take.

Regardless of the stand you choose, pay close attention to how level the aquarium is when placed on top of the stand. Companies that build such stands test them prior to shipment to your local aquarium shop, but it never hurts to check for yourself. After all, sometimes the stand may have been used to support other things that are far heavier than the weight the stand was initially rated for, or the stand may have come in contact with excessive moisture or temperature extremes. These are factors that can significantly affect the structural integrity of the stand.

Once you have positioned your stand and placed your aquarium on it, use a level to make sure the tank sits perfectly even on all sides. Leaning even slightly due to an uneven floor or the like can cause disaster to strike in the form of a cracked panel or broken seam on the aquarium. If the tank and stand are slightly uneven, place wooden shims or Styrofoam in the proper areas to offset the imbalance prior to adding any water. Some hobbyists have used Styrofoam as a cushion placed in between the tank and the

stand—just in case there are small inconsistencies that cannot be readily seen with the naked eye. Such a safety precaution is recommended, though not usually needed.

Once you have successfully placed the stand in the perfect location and have assured that your aquarium will sit evenly upon it, you can go about setting up the system. While actually filling the tank is not necessarily the next step, you can begin to add some water; this will allow the stand some time to adjust to the eventual weight of the tank that will be completely filled with water. It is common to hear the stand creak and make other small noises during the initial filling of the tank. Of course, if the creaks turn into cracks and so on, you may need to

Once the tank is in place, and is sure to be level, you can begin setting it all up.

Many guppy keepers use inside box filters in their setups.

of aquarium filters: hang-on power filters, inside box filters, undergravel filters, and sponge filters. Oh sure, there are several others (i.e., canister, fluidized bed, wet/dry types, etc.), but for multiple tank setups or simple guppy setups they are generally considered impractical with regard to both their physical design and how expensive they are to use.

Hang-On Power Filters

By far the most popular type of filters for causal hobbyists are the hang-on style of power filters. These units come in a huge assortment of sizes and styles, and there is one made for every size of an ordinary glass aquarium. For really large aquariums, multiple units are commonly used.

Since most guppy aquariums are small, say under 15 gallons (56 l), a small unit that has a flow of 100 to 150 gallons (378 to 567 l) per hour would be suitable. If your

rethink your plans and adjust for whatever happens. In any instance, such noises should cause you to make draining the aquarium your first priority and seeking the assistance of a qualified aquarium technician your second!

Filtration & Aeration

While it is certainly possible to keep guppies with no external air supply or functioning filtration unit, this is not a practical path to follow. Here, we will assume that you are planning on using some form of filtration or aeration equipment. Practically speaking, guppy keepers commonly use four basic types

Even though undergravel filters are considered "old technology," they are still used by some hobbyists today.

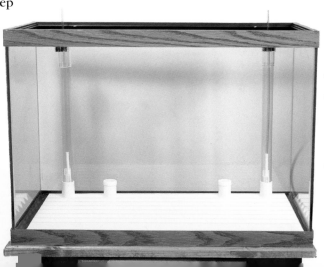

guppies have very long fins, then it's wise not to use these types of filters since the fish may get their fins caught in the filter's intake strainers and this will cause major health problems with the fish. While hang-on filters are the most common, they are not the best for guppy fanciers, so be sure to use them with caution.

Inside Box Filters

The box filter is just that, a small box that comes in various sizes and sits inside your tank. Probably the most commonly chosen type of filter by today's guppy breeders, these small box filters are air driven, that is, they require the force of pressurized air flowing through them in order to operate efficiently. The filter medium is usually filter floss and carbon or some other type of absorbent material. An airline is run down to the filter's pumping mechanism, at which point the filter

Diatom Filters

When aquariums become cloudy, some hobbyists employ a filter that uses diatomaceous earth to filter out fine particulates from the water. This type of filter will usually pump a hundred or more gallons of water in the course of an hour and can quickly remove most of the suspended particles in the tank. Hobbyists who use them say they have few, if any, problems with disease transference.

draws water down through the floss and then bubbles the air back into the tank. This type of filter has the added advantage of continuing to work even if the water level in the tank drops.

Undergravel Filters

The undergravel filter works primarily through bacterial action in combination with an external air supply. This type of filter is useful in keeping the water crystal clear in display tanks. Undergravel filters are fine for most other fish species, but generally considered to be useless for guppies. Breeders report that after using an undergravel filter for week or two, you will be able to watch the males' tails almost fall apart, due to a high bacteria count in their water. Although they may prove useful for a fish store, they are not a good choice for a serious guppy breeder.

Providing strong aeration in a guppy setup is never a bad idea.

Sponge Filters

Sponge filters are basically just a sponge with a combination siphon and air tube inside the sponge. They operate under the same basic bacterial-action principle as undergravel filters, but as a bonus, they provide a home to organisms such as rotifers and copepods which are treats small guppies love to feast upon. Their disadvantage is that they don't usually pick up a lot of mulm from the bottom of the tank, which will occasionally cause bacterial levels to get out of control, possibly causing fin and tail damage to the males. Some guppy breeders use them with good results but many simply use inside box filters instead.

Air Supply

An air pump, or compressor, has to provide a constant, oil-free supply of fresh air to the water in an aquarium, and do this in the most economical way. A powerful, piston-driven pump may be sufficient for some tanks. When purchasing one, however, it is wise to plan ahead and select a pump that is powerful enough for expansion needs, because guppy keepers always seem to add more tanks. You may also need an extra air supply if you choose to operate brine shrimp hatcheries in order to cultivate them as food for your fish.

It is good practice to locate the compressor on the floor with enough clear space around it so air can circulate adequately and cool the unit. Sometimes people wrap insulation

Hang-on heaters are common in guppy setups.

around the pump in an attempt to cut down on the noise some units make. This is not a good idea since this often results in a burned out motor.

Temperature Control

Using individual heaters for just a few tanks is feasible, but if you are going to run a number of tanks you are better off with an enclosed room that has a single heat source. You can use a small space heater (with proper ventilation and fire safeguards of course) or pump hot air into the room

24

from ducts leading from your furnace. The only problem this presents is how to maintain a constant temperature. Make sure all the walls and ceilings are properly insulated. Once the water temperature in all the tanks is raised to the correct level, it will not require too much heat to maintain these temperature levels continuously. Also, 220-V baseboard heaters that operate with a thermostat mounted on an inside wall opposite the aquariums are economical and effective.

You might find it necessary to bring fresh air into an enclosed room, as humidity can become quite high in fishrooms. One of the best ways to accomplish this is to use a PVC line that is hooked to the input line of an air compressor. In the warmer months, unless it's always warm where you live, you can draw fresh air in from outside.

When it turns cold, the inlet from the outside atmosphere can be turned off and air can be drawn in from other areas of the house instead. Alternately, you can use small box fans to bring in air from adjacent sources. These units really make fish rooms livable, as the air in them tends to get quite stuffy and terribly humid. Under extreme conditions it may be necessary to add an air-exchange unit to bring fresh air in and exhaust the moist stale air. This unit may also help to control mildew and fungus in the fish room.

If you use individual heaters, use caution when cleaning your tanks. It is very easy to break the outside layer of glass on this type of heater. If this happens, and the heater is on at the time, you will receive a very nasty shock when your hand comes in contact with the water in the aquarium.

Lighting

Many people assume that fish need overhead lighting on their aquariums. This is simply not true; in fact, most fish spend much of their time under branches, among rocks, or in thick vegetation in nature, so why would fish miraculously need light when kept in glass boxes? They don't. Lighting is important only if *you* want to grow plants or see into your aquarium. However, hobbyists still insist on installing lighting fixtures over their aquariums. This isn't necessarily a bad thing at all—as long as they have a little basic knowledge of the subject.

Incandescent Lighting

Basically, there are two different types of lights: fluorescent and incandescent. For an individual aquarium, incandescent lighting provides good plant growing possibilities but gives off a lot more heat compared to fluorescent bulbs. Additionally, although the initial purchase price is inexpensive, incandescent lighting is quite costly to run compared to the amount of light that it produces. Many people still do appreciate incandescent lighting sources for their aquariums, simply for the dim effects they can create. Since most fish shy away from bright light, using these dim lights may allow you to observe your fishes under a somewhat more natural setting—without the look of a spaceship landing in your room which is what fluorescent lighting resembles.

Fluorescent Lighting

Fluorescent fixtures are more expensive to purchase initially, but they last longer and are cooler and cheaper to operate. Generally, hobbyists use either warm-white, cool-white, or a combination of bulb types in their fluorescent fixtures. You may wish to use a warm-white to bring out the reds and oranges in your

Fluorescent tubes provide a wide array of lighting

Any substrate that is to be used in aquariums should be thoroughly rinsed before being placed in the tank.

guppies, or a cool-white daylight bulb to bring out the blues and greens. The number of bulbs needed over your aquarium will be determined by how bright you want your aquarium to be. Fish can be raised successfully under dim or bright lighting, but I have found that a moderate amount of light is best.

Substrate & Decorations

Gravel is an anathema for the guppy breeder. Gravel is definitely not your friend if you intend to raise or maintain show guppies in any quantity. However, if you plan to have a show tank with plants, rocks, bogwood, or other decorations, then gravel is fine as long as it is a fine, rounded type. Gravel with a course grain is completely unsuitable, as food will fall between the gravel pieces, creating tremendous water-quality problems. Additionally, gravel with sharp edges is also completely unsuitable as a substrate since fish can injure themselves on it.

Rinse the substrate thoroughly rinsed before placing it in the aquarium. This is best accomplished with warm water. After a thorough rinsing, pour the gravel poured into the aquarium in a uniform fashion.

If you do use gravel in your tanks, it is necessary to stir up the gravel on a regular basis. This is done so that uneaten food and debris cannot accumulate under the surface, which causes the water to foul and turn the gravel black and malodorous, thus wreaking havoc with the fish.

Most professional guppy breeders don't use any decorations or substrate at all. Why? Because substrate harbors bacteria and when the density of bacteria in an aquarium containing guppies rises too high, then the male's tails will begin to degenerate and flake apart. Decorations can cause a similar problem, especially if the tank is heavily decorated, as the décor can harbor high levels of bacteria. The best advice about substrate and decorations is to use them in moderation and always be sure to perform regular partial water changes and keep the filter as clean as possible at all times.

If you decide that you must use decorations and you add a substrate to your guppy tank, then you should know that the color or size of the gravel or sand does not make any difference. Some hobbyists speculate that because sand is finer it doesn't harbor as much bacteria. This is wrong. Actually, sand can harbor just as much bacteria as any type of gravel. Either way, keeping it clean, or absent altogether, are the best protocols.

Testing, Testing... 1, 2, 3

Unlike larger, more robust species, guppies can be sensitive to things like pH levels, water hardness, and chlorine levels in your aquarium. Other factors, like ammonia, nitrite, and nitrate are certain killers if their concentrations are allowed to rise to unsafe levels.

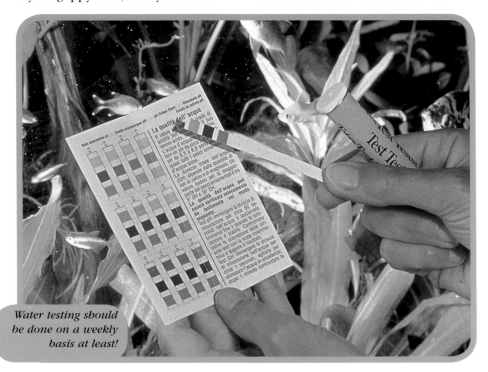

Water testing should be done on a weekly basis at least!

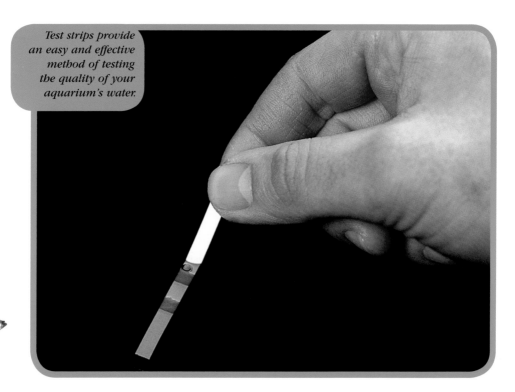

Test strips provide an easy and effective method of testing the quality of your aquarium's water.

pH

Most fish can tolerate a wide range of pH measurements as long as extremes are avoided and that the pH does not fluctuate, or swing, from one side of the scale to the other. The pH of a system is based on a number scale from 1 to 14. A measurement of 7 is considered neutral while anything lower is acidic and higher is basic, or alkaline. On average, guppies seem to do best in pH values ranging between 6.5 and 7.5.

Hardness (dH)

Measured in the German degree of hardness, or dH, hardness can be broken down further into general and carbonate hardness, or dGH and dKH respectively. None of these are overly important for guppy keeping, again, as long as extremes are avoided. Many hardness test kits offer a reading of "soft, moderate, or hard" on their scales because the quantitative measurements are rather hard to keep straight. On average, guppies seem to do well in water that measures "moderate." If you live in an area where the water is very hard, you should run the water through a softening filter before exposing guppies to it. For my

Proper Levels

Ammonia, nitrite, and nitrate are all measured in parts per million (ppm). While ammonia and nitrite should read as close to zero as possible, nitrate can be slightly elevated but should not be allowed to rise above 75 ppm. If it does, an immediate changing of approximately 50 percent of the aquarium's water is suggested, and regular water changes may be needed to keep the level below that. Remember, water changes are the key to a healthy aquarium and success with guppies.

poison and any water that goes into any aquarium should be devoid of it. When you test for chlorine, make sure its reading is at zero before placing fish in the water, as any exposure to it could mean death for the fish. Additionally, some people have mentioned that they have problems finding a good test kit for chlorine. If you are having the same difficulty, check with a garden pond supply store, they usually have them.

Ammonia, Nitrite & Nitrate

Ammonia, nitrite, and nitrate are toxic compounds excreted by the guppies themselves, as well as other fishes. Decaying food, plants, and other organic and inorganic materials will also cause levels of these substances to become elevated, too. While ammonia and nitrite should read zero, or as close to zero as possible, nitrate is another matter. Nitrate is toxic, but not nearly as toxic compared to the other two. One of the main problems associated with nitrate is that it's

own water conditions, I run the hot water supply through a water softening unit, and the cold water directly from the well. This combination still ends up as somewhat hard water, but it's acceptable for fish keeping.

Chlorine

This toxic compound is used to sterilize tap water. Basically, it's a

Keep it Covered!

If you look closely at your guppies, you'll see that they are almost flat across their backs. This unique feature allows them to cruise just beneath the water's surface in search of tiny insects that have just fallen into the water. This also means that they spend a lot of time near the surface of the water. Fishes that spend time at the top of aquariums tend to be accomplished jumpers so make sure that your aquarium has a tight-fitting lid.

SMALL FRY

is the reduced number of fish you will have to work with. With a well-established line, it is possible to raise fewer fish and still compete well at guppy shows if you choose to go that route later on.

The Basic Elements for Success

Here's a checklist of the basic elements for success with guppies:

1. A 5-gallon (19 l) aquarium minimum
2. A strong stand to place the tank on
3. An efficient filtration system
4. Sturdy cover (lighting optional)
5. Heater
6. This book!

The Tank

Add aged aquarium water and a used, fairly clean filter from a healthy, existing aquarium whenever setting up a new tank. Let the filter run for at least 24 hours and then add some plants, such as water sprite for example, which is a strong plant that does well in newly set up tanks. Also, water sprite has a tendency to act as an indicator—if the water sprite is doing well, then, usually, so are the guppies. When the water sprite starts to die, the tank's water

a fertilizer, and excessive amounts will often cause major outbreaks of algae, which in turn can lead to a high bacterial count. Guppies and elevated bacterial counts don't mix, especially with males, as their fins will decay and flake apart.

Setting Up & Maintenance

With most fishes, except for guppies, bettas, and killifishes, it is necessary to have large tanks for proper growth. When raising guppies, it is possible to produce good fish using only 5-gallon (19 l) aquariums. This makes it nice for those of us who have space problems. About the only drawback

Water changes should be performed on a regular basis.

quality usually is deteriorating. One of my tricks when I do want to use plants in a tank is to use small glass containers and root the plant right in the glass container. You can then add a few of these planted glass containers to your tank with no difficulty and, best of all, no gravel is needed. Both water sprite and Amazon swordplants seem to do very well in these types of setups. No matter how practical I try to be, from time to time I do succumb to my desire to see guppies swimming in a beautifully planted tank. In our drive to produce bigger and better fish, we sometimes forget to take the time to just sit back and enjoy our fish, which is very important to do.

Water Changes are a Must!

With young guppies, water changes up to 75 percent can be made without too much harm since young fish are often more adaptable and take change better. As guppies grow, smaller water changes are a safer bet. With older guppies that may or may not still be breeding, 10 to 15 percent water changes are recommended only once per week. In most cases, water changes are safe to perform as long as they are done regularly and that drastic extremes in water chemistry are avoided.

Water Changes & Water Quality

Water changes may be the most important topic in this whole book. And performing them is vital to maintaining water quality high enough for breeding and showing your guppies. Decades ago, the only water that was added to the aquarium was replacement for the water lost to evaporation. It was found that the fish originally in the tank remained healthy after the tank had been set up for a while, but when any new fish were added, they usually ended up sick or dead. What was occurring was the gradual build-up of concentrated salts and minerals that were lethal to the newly added fish.

The answer to this problem was simply draining water off the bottom of the tank, rather than just replacing that which had evaporated. Frequent siphoning reduces the salt and mineral content to an acceptable level.

With smaller tanks it may be necessary to change more water more often. There is no room for error as you would have with larger tanks. More attention to detail in feeding and filter management is also required in order to prevent any runaway change in pH and ammonia levels. Along with the increased water changes there is less impact on your fish from both of these factors. While closer observation and a little more work may be involved with the smaller tank setup, you can still do a good job with your fish.

Good water quality is extremely important for success with fancy guppies.

Conditioning New Water

It is not always necessary to add chemical additives to new water before it's added to the guppy aquarium. Hobbyists fortunate enough to have well water of good quality or even spring water available to them rarely need any additives at all—especially if the guppies are already acclimated to that environment. Occasionally, however, in some areas, water conditions are not conducive to keeping fishes—especially those where a significant amount of

chemicals are added to the water supply. In these instances it may be necessary to bring in water from another source. Normally, these problems can be controlled by filtering or softening the water.

Most instances in which guppies suffer from shock can probably be drastically reduced if proper time and effort is allowed for their initial acclimation. For example, if you have water that is extremely hard and maintains a pH of around 8.5, then you'll have a difficult time keeping guppies that are accustomed to living in a neutral-water aquarium. However, if enough

time and dedication is allowed, nearly all types of fishes, including guppies, can be acclimated to other, perhaps less desirable, water chemistries.

Hobbyists who unfortunately have a poor supply of water will just have to watch the amount and frequency of water changes. It is universally considered a waste of time and effort to try to maintain a constant pH level, at least for raising guppies. Guppies must become acclimated to your specific conditions rather than having you try to maintain artificial ones for them.

Unless you intend to write a scientific paper many pages long on the chemical makeup of water and its supposed advantages and disadvantages for your guppies, why worry too much about them? Just set up a workable, easy-to-use, and reliable method of changing your guppies' water, and then adhere to it. If you are setting up a tank for the first time and if no conditioned water or a matured filter pad is available to you, you can start off almost as well by using some stress-reducing (for you) and "instant cycling" additives (for your fish) to your water. While using fish-conditioned water would be best, instant cycling some water is better than drawing raw water

Guppies love clean aquariums!

right from the tap. The trick? Just add a couple of cory cats to the new tank set up;, they will assist in conditioning the water before you add the guppies.

Cleaning the Tank

Cleaning the entire aquarium is quite simple. To break it down completely, drain all of the water out, remove any equipment and decorations, and most importantly, then you have to remove the guppies. It should be noted, however, that the fish are far easier to catch *after* all the accessories and decorations have been removed from the aquarium and the water level has been reduced, which leaves them no place to swim and hide.

After the aquarium is empty, clean it out with a gallon of warm water to which you have added a strong saline solution. This will act as a disinfectant without leaving a chemical residue. Using a nylon sponge pad, scrub the tank completely, paying particular attention to the corners and seams. After the tank is clean, rinse it several times with clean water before you set it back up.

Supplies to Keep on Hand

All of the tools and gadgets used to help maintain other fishes housed in tanks are valuable for the guppy aquarium, too. Thermometers, feeding rings, powerhead filters, air pumps, nets, siphons, and test kits—they all have their place. Thermometers and siphons are essential, of course, but a ton of other things out there may have no use to you unless you have other aquariums that contain other fishes besides guppies.

Chapter 3

Good Eating

Probably the most important factor concerning food for guppies is whether or not the guppies will actually accept what you are offering them. I realize that sounds somewhat simplistic, since if you were to starve them for a long period of time, they would probably eat just about anything you would put in front of them, but on a day-to-day basis, it is necessary to provide them with palatable foods that will entice them to eat more, even when their stomachs are partially full.

An active guppy can probably eat every hour or so. But if various foods they eat appeal to their taste buds, they will continue to feed even though they are not really hungry. That's like us trying to eat just one potato chip.

Commercial Foods

Throughout the years, I have fed my fish all types of commercial and non-commercial fish foods. Some of the commercial guppy foods are pretty good and some are merely just a little better than no food at all. There are a lot of foods that would be good for your fish, but because fish are cold-blooded (their body temperature is the same as the water), these foods will not break down properly and will thus pass through their digestive systems intact, and so you are forced to use food groups that can be assimilated. It's your choice as to

The Expert Knows

Clean Hands

One important point for the fancy guppy keeper is to always make sure that your hands are clean when you are feeding your fish or servicing their aquarium. If your hands are not clean, you can accidentally introduce some harmful substance and then wonder why your fish are sick. Substances like soap, perfume, or hand moisterizer lotion may be toxic to fishes. One of the best ways to make sure that your hands are free of toxic substances is to rub them together under hot water.

whether it is best for you to blend your own food mixtures or to use ready-made foods. Fish food manufacturers generally put better-quality ingredients in higher-priced foods, so you may want to remember that when you go shopping for fish foods. Don't try to save a few cents by buying lower quality foods, since poor-quality foods may cost you more in the long run if they cause problems.

Commercial flaked foods are among the easiest of all types of foods to feed guppies.

Small pellets are sometimes taken by large guppies but flakes are usually a better alternative.

Is there one single type of dry food that has all the necessary nutrients and vitamins for a completely balanced guppy diet? That is a loaded question, but one that deserves some attention. Basically, professionals out there feel that if you provide a variety of foods to your fish then you'll be providing them with the proper nutrients. Very few settle on just one brand, let alone one type of food. If you doubt any manufacturer's claim that any particular product is an "all-in-one" food, then do a little see-for-yourself testing by separating a few guppies and feeding them nothing but one brand and one type of food for no less than two weeks. The answer may surprise you—or it may not.

Dry Foods

One of the best things you can do for your guppies is to present them with a staple diet consisting of a wide variety of good-quality dry foods. When feeding dry foods, use a fine or medium-fine grade food, as the particles must be small enough for the fish to ingest. If you use flake food, it's a good idea to crush it between your fingers—especially when feeding it to baby guppies.

Lock Up the Food

Because guppies can be gluttons, and children love to feed fish, it's wise to keep fish food out of reach of young children. They may be tempted to feed them, and then feed them some more, and more, and before you know it, the tank is a smelly mess and the guppies are no longer the happy little fish they used to be. Your maintaining control of the fish food is a good way to teach children the responsible way to feed not only fish, but all pets in general.

Overfeeding

Several years back, an experiment was done on a tank full of young female guppies. It started as offering them a slight feeding of dry food—just enough to partially satisfy their appetites. Food was offered again a few minutes later and this second feeding continued for a total of thirty minutes. During this time, the fish became so worked up that the water appeared as if it were boiling while the guppies were aggressively trying to get at the food. Even though their stomachs became greatly distended, they still wanted to eat more. The experiment was stopped when several of the females dropped to the bottom of the tank—they were dead.

So what did this prove? Perhaps only that the way that you feed, combined with the quality of the food being fed, determines the growth pattern. It would be nice to retain this triggered response in all of your fish at feeding time, but it doesn't work that way. Without belaboring the point, any time fish do not come to the front of the tank to feed, do not give them any food, no matter what you think they may need. Even if it becomes necessary for them to go a day or two without any feeding, they will be better off for it.

Several forms of dry food are commonly available: flakes, pellets, granules, wafers, and powders. Of those listed, only flakes and very small pellets are really of any use for guppies, as the others usually come in forms that are too large for guppies to consume effectively without excess waste.

Frozen Foods

Adding some frozen and fresh types of foods will benefit your guppies greatly—and they'll appreciate the diversity in their diet. Today, more than ever before, hobbyists have a huge array of frozen fish foods at their disposal. Many of them are for specialty situations, such as maintaining fish in seawater aquariums, and for feeding

Frozen bloodworms make an excellent addition to a guppy's diet.

fish with special feeding needs such as stingrays or discus, but a good number of frozen foods are suitable for guppies, too. Try to stay away from foods that look too large for guppies to eat. Brine shrimp, mysis shrimp, bloodworms, tubifex worms, and copepods are probably the best of whatever is available out there, but some of the "community" formulas are good as well. Try different brands and mixtures to see what works best for you.

Freeze-Dried Foods

The vast majority of freeze-dried foods are too large for guppies to feast upon. However, if you grind them up they will work wonderfully, and these foods provide a wide array of nutrients that are hard to obtain from other sources. The most common types are: krill; cubes of tubifex worms and brine shrimp;, large plankton; grass shrimp; and crickets. Bloodworms are available from time to time and make a great addition to a guppy's diet. Additionally, formulas that

Some freeze-dried foods can be pressed up against the glass for the fish to easily feed upon.

Guppies Love Bugs!

In nature, guppies feed primarily on insect larvae and small surface-dwelling water insects. In aquariums, this diet can be replicated by offering the guppies wingless fruit flies, which are available from your local pet shop.

other crustaceans; beef liver and other specialized meat meals; kelp; some form of cereal meal (to add consistency to the food formulations); spirulina; and various yeasts; along with an array of vitamin and mineral supplements that are readily available at local health food stores. I realized a long time ago that it was too labor intensive and almost impossible to recreate foods that fish would feed upon in the wild.

Live Foods

Baby brine shrimp are the safest live foods to use for feeding guppies. Initially, I had thought it was necessary to feed additional live foods to compliment the dry foods for good growth. But in my own case, all the extra work in obtaining the live food, along with the possibility of introducing disease to my tanks, made it unattractive.

Tubifex Worms

Tubifex worms are probably one of the best foods you can use to

come in small wafer-type shapes are sometimes available through your local pet shop. These work well and are easy to use. Simply place the wafer under water for a few seconds then press it against the wall of the aquarium. After a while, the guppies will swim over to it and begin to pick it apart.

Non-Commercial Foods

You can easily keep fish healthy for many years if you just use only fish foods that are commercially prepared and marketed. Nevertheless, home processed foods are other options.

Homemade Foods

Most popular forms of specially created homemade fish foods consist of fish and fish-liver meals; shrimp (with shells) and

Tubifex Worms

encourage serious growth in your guppies, or any other fishes for that matter, but be careful when handling the worms and feeding them to your fish. These worms require special storage conditions: The water they are in needs to be constantly refreshed and they are actually best kept in water that is constantly running over them. They can also be kept cool in a refrigerator, but only for short periods of time. I have seen some exceptionally nice guppies raised on tubifex worms, but I have also seen a number of guppy raisers put out of business because of them.

White Worms

White worms foster body growth, but shouldn't be fed to fish more than twice weekly. Overfeeding can cause a buildup of fatty deposits in the fishes' body, resulting in an extremely bloated condition and ruined fish.

Daphnia

Daphnia are also a fairly good to be used as fish food. Their protein content is quite low, but the fish seem to enjoy chasing them, and the roughage they provide is beneficial for the fish.

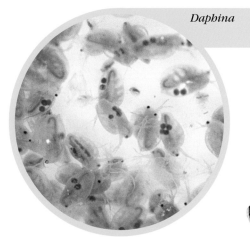

Daphina

Mosquito Larvae

Mosquito larvae are an excellent food for guppies, and they are an item that fish feed upon most often in nature.

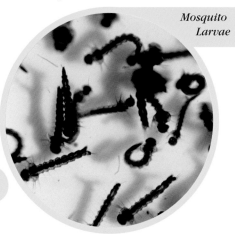

Mosquito Larvae

White Worms

The one and only time that I used them in my fishroom, however, the fish didn't eat all of them and as an end result, I wound up being chased around the room by adult mosquitoes!

Brine Shrimp

Both adult and baby brine shrimp are an excellent food to offer guppies. While not the most nutritional live foods, they do offer hobbyists the ability to use them as a vehicle for delivering additives like spirulina or bee pollen to their guppies. This, in turn, makes them very useful and a sometime necessary food if you want to keep your guppies in tip-top condition.

Brine Shrimp

Fancy Guppies

SMALL FRY

Spice Things Up

Guppies sometimes get bored with their food. To spice things up for them, always try new foods, even different brands of the same types of foods. For example, whenever you're cruising the isles of your local pet shop searching for a new dog bone or cat toy, also pick up a new type of food for your guppies. There are many types of foods that will offer your guppies something different to eat while adding a new selection of nutrients they might need—what could be better?

Feeding Your Guppies

For the first feeding of the day, give the fish just a small amount of dry food. After a few minutes, go back and give them a second round of just a pinch more of dry food. Once in a while, especially when feeding many guppies, give them a third round in the morning.

If offering live foods, like baby brine shrimp or daphnia for example, they can now be fed to the guppies—usually enough for them to feed on for a few hours. At this time, you can give the guppies that did not get any shrimp another offering of dry food, but remember not to overdo it with the dry food and make sure they come up to the front glass to get it.

Healthy, well-fed guppies should have a nice rounded-out appearance.

In the late afternoon, or early evening, feed the guppies another couple of offerings of dry food. About three times a week, all of the fish, except the very young babies, should be fed frozen adult brine shrimp (which have been thawed of course). After the frozen food has thawed, pour the contents through a net and rinse under cool water to remove excess small particles that would only just pollute your tank anyway. Feed them all they will eat without leaving any leftovers.

Overfeeding is a Problem!

Only feed the amount of food needed to slightly round off your fish's bellies. Overfeeding can cause a huge array of water-quality problems, which all lead to health issues. If you find that some of the food floats around the aquarium for several minutes—only to be sucked into the filter—then you are certainly overfeeding. The only exception to this is when offering live baby brine shrimp to your young guppies. They simply cannot eat them all right away but in time they will. Unlike flaked or other dry foods, live baby brine shrimp will not rot and cause major issues right away. Of course, if enough baby brine shrimp are given, then they can certainly cause major problems but as with anything, moderation is the key.

Chapter 4

Feeling Good

People have very little control over their own environment, but as a hobbyist, that which you exercise over your fishroom is almost total. You provide all the food, water, lighting, level of temperature, and to a great extent, the amount of oxygen available in the water. So if your fish develop problems, you usually don't have to look too far for the guilty person.

Normally, fish kept in good tank conditions, with clean filters, and fed a well-balanced diet, contract very few diseases. Overfeed them a couple of times, get lax on water and filter changing protocols, and you will suddenly have problems.

You cannot slap a bandage on a fish, but keeping the water clean with frequent water changes will lower the bacterial count, and a tablespoon of salt per every five gallons will help by increasing the fish's slime coat to protect the wound. Basically, you should just keep an eye on the injury until it is healed, but nothing needs to be done unless it develops signs of infection.

Injuries

Guppies can be injured by rough handling, sharp objects in the tank, or fin-nipping tankmates, since many more of them are kept in home aquariums in relation to their fancy guppies neighbors. Cuts and bruises are for guppies much the same as they are for us: minor injuries that will heal quickly unless they become infected.

Illness

How can you tell when your guppies are sick? The best way to be alert to signs of illness is to be very familiar with the way your fish look and act like when they are well. If you do, then a sudden negative change in a fish's appearance or behavior can be indicative of disease. By a negative change I mean your fish suddenly seems listless, has lost some color, clamped his fins, or has strange spots on the body. Spotting these developments as symptoms of illness, therefore, depends on your knowledge of your fish in their healthy condition.

Recognizing Symptoms

With all guppies, one of the first symptoms of disease is a general listlessness and lack of interest in food. When you feed them dry food, if something is wrong with them, they will usually swim under the food without attempting to take it, and will only pick lightly at live foods such as live brine shrimp. At this point, the fish and the entire aquarium should be closely examined. If nothing seems to be wrong with the tank, filter, and no visual problem with the fish can be seen, the best thing to do is to stop feeding the fish in this tank for several days. If there is no major problem, they will snap out of it and be well again. On the other hand, if you fail to observe a serious illness and continue to drop food in the tank, you stand a good chance of losing a large portion or all of the fish in the tank. After several days, the fish will start to get

The first sign of disease with any fish is a general listlessness and refusal to eat.

thin in the body and from this point on they will gradually deteriorate until they die.

The best way to keep guppies healthy is to avoid all forms of excess, whether in temperature range, amount and type of food offered, or water quality. Don't chill or overheat the guppies; don't overfeed the guppies; don't subject them to contamination by exposing them to other sick fish; don't crowd them; don't let pollutants build up in their tanks. Follow that regimen, and you should have very few disease problems to handle. Treat guppies well and they'll reward you with years and years of fascination and perhaps even a few thousand babies; treat them badly and they'll only give you back the same kind of grief you gave them.

The fancy-tailed guppies that we all try to develop and perfect are a far cry from the wild guppy in natural habitats. The wild guppy, with its small caudal fin, does not have a problem with its blood supply reaching the outer edges of the caudal fin as our fancy-tailed strains do. An inadequate blood supply will cause a weakening and gradual breakdown of tissue, which invites bacterial infection. There is a natural slime coating on the fish which protects it from many diseases. If, through carelessness, we let the tank go bad, which in turn causes a bacterial buildup, a chain-like reaction occurs as the fish's defense mechanism breaks down, leaving the fish in a weakened condition and susceptible to any prevalent disease.

Fin & Tail Rot

Fin and tail rot, a bacterial infection of the fins, is by far the most common ailment that will infect your guppies and is mostly associated with guppies that are kept in aquariums that are laden with bacteria. There are ways to lesson the likelihood of this disease, one of which is to cut

Overfeeding Revisited

Overfeeding will cause a bacterial build up and also increase the ammonia content. Normally, if you do not overcrowd your fish and maintain scheduled water changes, ammonia is not a problem.

down on the amount and frequency of feedings. This will hinder the possible imbalance of the bacterial level in the tank. Other ways to retard bacterial growth are by lowering the temperature and removing the slime that grows on the inside walls of aquariums.

It is important to know that you don't want to destroy *all* the bacteria in the tank but rather just keep them down to reasonable levels. Beneficial bacteria, like those responsible for converting harmful wastes into less harmful by-products, will not negatively affect your fish's health, but you don't want an

The long-flowing fins of guppies are especially vulnerable to fin rot.

over abundance of them either, since that will indicate that you have too much waste material present in your tank.

The use of salt will promote the maintenance of the protective slime coating on the fish bodies but is of little help in preventing fin and tail rot.

Columnaris

This disease is usually associated with female guppies, and the symptoms look similar to a fungal infection. It usually manifests itself in spots or as areas that lack pigmentation—especially in the peduncle region. If left unchecked, it can spread throughout the tank with a very high killing ratio. It is bacterial in nature, and from my own observations, is caused by unclean tank or filter conditions. Further manifestation of the disease may be a gradual paralyzing of the body itself. It is also possible that some foods may promote the growth of this infectious bacterium, and those suspected most are the ones with a high organic base ingredient or those high in gelatin, which is used as a binder.

The Expert Knows

Salt

Salt remains one of the best treatments for fish ailments. Most freshwater fish can tolerate some salt in their water, and guppies can usually tolerate more than many other fishes can, but most fish pathogens cannot. Salt also increases a fish's slime coat, which helps the fish to ward off parasites like ich. Salt should never be overdosed, and it's important to know that salt will not evaporate with water either. Therefore, only treat the whole tank with salt one time and then for only the volume of water removed after each water change thereafter.

Ick/Ich

Ich or ick, named for *Ichthyophthirius multifiliis*, the parasite that causes it, is probably the only fish ailment you can easily identify and treat. Make no mistake, this is a potentially deadly disease with a possible mortality rate of 100 percent, but if caught immediately, the survival rate can also be 100 percent. Some fish are

Feeling Good

Young guppies are very prone to ich outbreaks.

much more prone to the affliction than others, but any species of fish is susceptible to it. You must treat all the fish in the tank, as the disease is highly contagious.

The diagnostic symptom of ich is the presence of the parasites embedded in the skin of the fish. They appear as little white bumps, giving the fish the appearance of having been salted. It is important to remember that these parasites also embed themselves in the gills as well as on the skin and fins of the fish.

The only time that the parasites are susceptible to treatments is when they are freeswimming. The rest of the time they are encapsulated and protected from chemicals.

The speed of the life cycle depends on temperature and can be greater than a month. At tropical aquarium temperatures, it is less than a week.

This is why the first course of treatment is to raise the temperature of the water. At about 80°F (27°C) the life cycle takes only a couple of days. This means that a new batch of freeswimming parasites will hatch out every two days, and they can be killed at this point.

A temperature of 90°F (32°C) will kill the freeswimming parasites. Most tropical fish can tolerate this temperature for the week to 10 days it will take to completely wipe out the ich infestation. Remember, though, that water this hot has a very limited capability of carrying dissolved oxygen, so increase the water flow dramatically. Ich compromises a fish's gills, increasing its need for oxygen even more.

There are several chemical preparations that are effective in treating ich outbreaks. You can purchase these at your aquarium

Swelling of the Chest

Another condition that sometime affects guppies, particularly males, is a condition where the chest area swells. This is usually caused by fatty deposits within the body cavity itself. In some cases it will develop to the point where the chest actually splits open, causing death. A very rich diet seems to be the culprit. Once the fish reach a certain point it seems irreversible. They continue to remain active and eating until they die, and it doesn't at all seem to be contagious, but it is a good idea to remove any dead fish as soon as you notice them.

retailer, and you should follow the label instructions carefully, especially as to dosage. Remember that a single treatment cannot eliminate ich, since by the time the next batch of parasites hatches out, the medication will be degraded.

No matter what treatment you select, you should vacuum the tank bottom at least once a day. This

Overcrowding can lead to bent spines or other deformities, so be sure to always provide enough room for the guppies to grow and thrive.

removes a great many of the incubating parasites before they can hatch out into their freeswimming stage.

Fish Stress Factors

Stress can be caused by a number of factors: the bacterial level in the aquarium could become unbalanced due to overfeeding; water quality could become unhealthy due to poor husbandry practices and lack of sufficient water changes; or the filter could become ineffective due to maintenance that is either too frequent or too infrequent.

Overcrowding

In raising your guppies, there is a tendency to crowd them somewhat, as you normally start them off in a small tank and move them up into larger ones from there. Always make sure they have adequate living space. Also, you may keep them at a slightly higher temperature to increase activity and make them eat more. So you would need to supply an additional amount of air to increase the level

Guppies kept in crowded holding tanks are especially prone to a wide assortment of diseases and other problems.

of dissolved oxygen in the higher-temperature water in the aquarium.

Balance is the Key

As long as you maintain the proper balance, everything should proceed very well. But if, for instance, you skip a water change or overfeed, you could be in for trouble. First of all you will have additional waste materials from the fish that were not removed. Secondly, any uneaten food will increase the ammonia level. The higher temperature will also decrease the oxygen content, which will enhance the ammonia buildup. With the increased ammonia concentration, the fish's tissue becomes more sensitive to the intrusion of the bacteria, which in turn can cause fin rot or other secondary infections as well as internal problems. Once this has gotten out of hand it is somewhat hard to rectify. The best solution is to change the fish to another tank. With older guppies, just stop feeding them for a

Teaching Respect for Living Beings

Trying to keep fish healthy teaches a child that all living creatures can suffer, and that we should do everything we can to alleviate their suffering. Children have an innate concern for other creatures, and a home aquarium can help them develop this attribute.

few days and the problems should even out on their own.

Odd Behavior

Occasionally, an individual guppy will become upset for some reason or other and any movement in front of the tank will cause him to dash to the most distant area of the aquarium away from you. Here he will hover with fins spread and body quivering. The other fish will often ignore him, but after a while such behavior may infect them, too. Soon after this you will have a whole tank full of of frightened, non-eating guppies. Just what triggers this reaction in an individual fish is hard to say. It would seem that some fish are similar to hyperactive humans and any slight stress factors cause them to flip out, so to speak. It is advisable to

A Note of Caution on Medications

All types of medications should be kept up and out of reach of children. Care should be taken when dealing with any medication. Do not get it into your eyes or breathe the fumes directly from the bottle. Make it a habit to always wash your hands thoroughly before and after handling medications—especially those that contain dyes.

Treating guppies for disease should be done in a separate quarantine aquarium whenever possible.

move slowly and not make any fast, jerky movements around your fish. When I run into this situation I usually isolate this fish immediately to prevent this chain reaction from happening. Sometimes, when multiple fish show these signs, withholding food for a few days will bring them out of it.

The fish themselves will usually let you know when they are sick or not feeling well. The main thing to do is keep your eyes open and then take the necessary action to rectify the problem before it gets out of hand.

Disease Treatment & Prevention

With certain diseases it becomes almost necessary to remove the fish from the tank to treat them. For practical purposes, it is not feasible to treat a whole tank of fish when only a couple of them have problems. In treating a case of fin rot, for example, the fish should be netted and the infected area treated using a cotton swab dipped in a strong solution of methylene blue or a weak solution of silver nitrate or copper sulfate. Care should be taken, however, that nothing gets into the gill or eye area of the guppy being treated. In some instances it may become necessary to trim off the infected area by using a razor blade.

Occasionally, genetic weaknesses are involved with certain strains of fish. No matter how ideal your tank conditions are, these fish will develop disease symptoms. If, after a generation or two, no improvement is noted, I would either bring in some new blood for a cross breeding or simply select another strain to work with.

Although the treatment of some diseases have already been touched on, it's important to focus on a few factors that are very important in treating sick fishes in general. The most important thing to keep in mind when caring for fish is to keep them healthy. To do this, you should focus your efforts on preventing diseases and problems from happening in the first place. Hobbyists should not have to medicate their aquariums on a regular basis, but they should have a basic understanding of how to recognize a disease and when to get some medication for a sick fish. To do this, you don't have to be a veterinarian but you should consult with someone who is knowledgeable.

Pet shops, aquarium wholesalers, local veterinarians, public aquariums, and research institutions usually have a professional on staff who is proficient in the treatment of fish diseases. But before you treat a disease, you must identify it, and identify it properly. This in and of itself is very problematic and beginners or even experienced hobbyists are not advised

to treat anything unless it has been positively identified and approved by a professional.

If, and when, your guppies get sick and you find out exactly what type of problem they have, be sure to administer any medications required to treat the problem strictly according to the manufacturer's advice. Any variation on this and you could turn one potential problem (the sick fish) into another problem entirely (a dead fish). This all being said, if you feel that your guppies are sick, it might be wise to consult a local professional for the proper methods in which to treat the problem.

Occasionally, when mixing strains of males in the same tank one strain will

Feeling Good

Patience is a Virtue

All too often in treating our fish we tend to use the headache/ aspirin approach. We assume that once a tank has been medicated, the fish should be cured in a matter of hours or at the least a day or two. It is important to realize that some diseases are slow to respond to medication and therefore it may be necessary to treat the tank several times in order to contain and eliminate any disease.

The author tends to crowd his males of one strain in the same tank. Thus, the need for cleanliness is essential.

get sick while the other strains remain healthy. This would lead one to think that there is an inherited factor involved. In reality it is simply that one line cannot handle a stress situation and falls prey to one of the disease or parasitic conditions present in the tank.

Quarantine Your Guppies!

Whenever possible, quarantine any newly acquired guppies before adding them to your stock. This will help ensure that any diseases or disorders will become apparent before it's too late and other fishes have been subjected to the infected fish. Quarantine aquariums don't have to be extensive and in fact it's better if they're not. For guppies, all you'll need is a 5-gallon (19 l) aquarium for their quarantine period, which should be at least seven days.

Chapter 5

Who Am I ?

One visit to a pet shop that sells fancy guppies, or a guppy breeder's hatchery, will instantly document that there are a tremendous variety of guppies available: greens, golds, blues, albinos, the varieties go on and on. In the end, for the average guppy fancier the quality of the guppy is basically decided on just two factors: the color of the guppy and whether or not it produces healthy offspring.

The Many Faces & Many Races of Guppies

The International Fancy Guppy Association (IFGA), the largest and most respected guppy club in the world, recognizes 26 classes of color and color combinations across several guppy categories (i.e., Tank, Delta, Breeders, Veil Tail, and Female). What follows is a brief description of just a sample of these classes. For more information, please refer to their website at www.ifga.org.

Red

Some of the most striking guppies commonly available are the reds. They are generally very colorful and hardy. The red strains seem to be well-established and are fairly easy to keep pure. Sometimes, the red guppies will actually appear pinker in color, which is fine as long as the rest of their traits are acceptable. This strain comes highly recommended for beginners to work with guppies and learn more about them.

Blue

Guppies that are predominately blue in both body and fin color are referred to as blue guppies. As with many types of fancy guppies, there is an assortment of variations on this strain. Occasionally, green iridescence will show up in the caudal fins of some blues, which makes for a very pleasing display.

Fancy Guppies

The Expert Knows

Male or Female, How Can I Tell?

The differences in male and female guppies are not totally apparent to newcomers and young hobbyists at first but with a little practice it becomes a very easy thing to distinguish. Basically, a male guppy has a pointed anal fin while a female guppy has a fanned out anal fin with a gravid spot. In some instances, however, a female of very high show quality may actually appear as a male guppy.

Green

Green guppies are one of the most difficult strains to maintain, but also one of the most rewarding due to their large flowing caudal fins that display shades ranging from a mint green to a deep forest green.

Purple

These interesting fish with an almost a velvet appearance show different shades of purple ranging from a pale violet to a deep purple color.

Black

An ideal black guppy would have an all black body with matching caudal and dorsal fins. Many breeders have attempted to bring the black coloration forward to include the head of the fish, usually with disastrous results, as there seems to be a lethal factor involved.

Multi

Basically, any guppy that has three or more colors in their body and fins is considered a multi. Most common examples in the pet trade are the blue/red combinations, but recently there has been an influx of yellow and red as well as green and red specimens, too.

Half-Black Red

These are some of the most spectacular guppies. The dorsal fins are usually a brilliant red, as are the caudal fins. The front half of the bodies ideally should show a lot of red but the entire back half is jet black with a tinge of blue iridescence.

Half-Black Blues

These fish have been around for some time and do very well at the shows. Every few generations, the females develop outstanding sized and colored caudal fins, many times equally matching the males in development.

Half-Black Pastel

With more muted colors, this half-black bodied fish shows a light shade of any basic color in its caudal fin. Some of the most striking show a light cream color in the dorsal and caudal fins.

Half-Black Purple

These fish have the same caudal fin colors of the regular purples, but since they have a half-black body, this makes a nice combination.

Snakeskin Variegated

This fish shows the same snakeskin markings in the body as the solid strain, but the caudal fins can also be a variegated color.

The Snakeskin Guppy

The snakeskin guppy is probably the most popular of all patterns. In the Orient, they are referred to as mosaic but in the United States and most other English-speaking countries they are more appropriately called snakeskin guppies.

Swordtails

There are three basic types of swordtail guppies: top sword, bottom sword, and double sword. The top sword is closest to the "wild-type" of the swordtailed strains, but double swords are popular, too. Just as their names describe them, a top-sword guppy has a pointed extension along the upper lobe of the caudal fin. The bottom-sword strain has one along the lower lobe of the caudal fin, and the double sword has a pointed extension on both the upper and lower lobes.

Some of these guppies are readily available through specialized breeders.

Snakeskin Solid

This striking fish has at least 60 percent of its body covered in a snakeskin pattern, complemented by any solid color in the caudal and dorsal fin areas.

Veil-tails

These male guppies display a tail spread of between 45-55 degrees.

Albino

Guppies with red or pink eyes are referred to as albinos. This is a hard strain to fix but once established they breed true. Just like their colored counterparts, albinos come in many types and even some have been crossed with other strains. For example, a red albino delta is a beautiful strain of fancy guppy. Another is the strikingly beautiful gold albino delta tail guppy.

Delta Tails

This guppy strain is referred to as delta tails because of the shape of their tails. Generally, a delta-tailed guppy has a tail that looks similar to that of a Greek letter delta shape, or triangle. Delta tails come in many strains, such as the blue deltas, green deltas, purple deltas, and so on.

Bronze

Any colored caudal is acceptable, but the body must have an old gold color with a minimum of 25 percent of scales darkly edged.

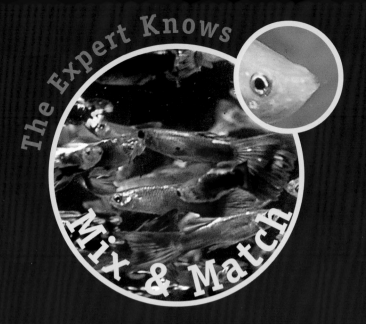

Mix & Match

Often, those interested in guppies are looking to maintain several types together. This is perfectly acceptable, as they will get along very well together and only rarely will there be battles among them. In fact, many hobbyists try to collect males of each strain and put together fancy guppy display aquariums with them. This works out well as long as females are left out of the equation, as males will compete ferociously for the right to mate with any female that is present.

Chapter 6

Breeding Guppies

Many years ago, information on breeding guppies was rather vague or misleading. In fact, it was even hard to find any information at all to begin with. You had to read everything available on the subject and ask many different fish folks questions that they often could not, or would not, answer. So many beginning hobbyists just started going their own way without being too concerned about what types of guppies would result from a cross.

My initial fish were from a couple of fish stores in the Detroit area; they were what you would now probably classify as semi-fancy guppies. Occasionally, a veiltail or modified wide-tailed male would crop up among the young, but this was a rare case. Within a few generations, the males started to look quite similar, with their caudal fins becoming more uniform in shape. However, there was still quite a variation in caudal color. The basic color was a red variegated pattern. Occasionally, I would get an off-color male with a greenish, blue, or even black variation. After about seven generations, a gold male popped up in one of the broods. He was bred with his daughter, and finally with his granddaughter. This was how my gold strain was fixed. About the same

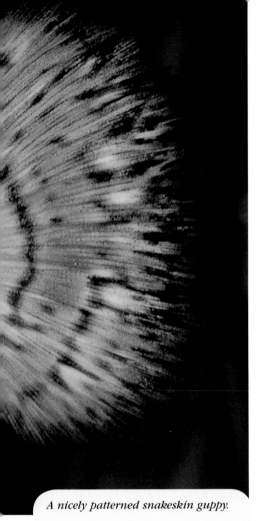

A nicely patterned snakeskin guppy.

bred for approximately 21 generations. Then, by using the females primarily for crossing the other lines, males with very wide tails, some with angles over 100 degrees, way beyond the super delta requirements, were developed.

Breeding Techniques

My normal breeding setup consists of two males and three to four females. The reason for this is the possibility of one of the males being sterile. In this case, you could sit there for a few months watching female after female ripen with unfertilized eggs and dropping no young. Most of the time they will just cast these out, but they have been known to reabsorb them occasionally, too. Only if a male is truly exceptional will he be used alone with a small group of females and then he will be watched closely to see that young are in fact forthcoming. When purchasing stock, try to obtain at least two trios of guppies, two males and four females.

The fish should be placed in a 5- or 10-gallon (19 to 38 l) tank. But wait to pick the breeders until they are between four and five months of age, the reason being that with some of the males, the caudal fins develop extending lobes as they get older. So wait until it can be determined that the caudal fins are developing fairly evenly along the trailing edges. Basically, it is a good idea to breed for one thing at a time—by this I mean that if you are breeding for size, use the largest fish; if you are breeding for color, use the best-colored males.

time, I took a couple of the off-colored males and started breeding them. The best way to do this was to cross the son back with the mother and then with one of the best females of the resulting drop.

In this manner, the reds, blues, greens, blacks, variegated, and partially black strains and even my original red variegated line became fixed and were

Pintails are not as popular in the United States as they are in the Orient.

The Breeding Stock

It is quite easy to look at a tank of males and pick out the best two or three fish. By best, it's implied that the ones who fill the requirements of the type of fish that you are trying to develop. Remove these males and place them in a breeding tank. Normally, it's best to leave them alone for a full day so they can establish their territories. For guppies, this means for them to simply feel at home in their new surroundings. The next day, the females can be added to the male's tank. This procedure can be followed for all setups. If the females are introduced before the males, they will often pick on the males fins and this may cause damage or infection to the male's tail. It seems that the first fish put in the tank has pecking precedence over those put in later.

Picking the females is very important, and some extra time and effort should be spent in doing so. It is here where many breeders run into trouble because they simply don't know what characteristics to look for in a good-quality female guppy. If this is not done properly, all you can do after a couple of generations is go back

Guppies that are to be bred in the future should be given separate quarters to allow their fins to grow out.

and get some more breeding stock. A lot of breeders cross everything and occasionally come up with some good fish, but again they are unable to hold the line with them.

Each strain may vary somewhat, but generally speaking what I look for are females with a compact rather than an elongated body—the peduncle area of a good thickness—and a generally well-shaped body overall. Next, check the tails, some color is desired—usually that which is evenly distributed. Try to pick those with the widest separation between the fin rays, and yet at the same time maintaining an even tail shape.

For those raising females for show purposes, it will be found that the gaudy or brightly colored females will not, as a rule, throw very good males. In fact, some of the nicest-finned females will throw nothing but poor quality males when bred, even if bred to a very high quality male.

About the only time you would use clear-tailed females for breeding is when dealing with swordtail guppies. When working with delta-tailed strains, you get very few clear-tailed females. Occasionally, when working with half-

black reds, you will get regular gray females; these are good to use along with the half-black females for breeding.

Probably the hardest lines to maintain are the albinos. Next most difficult are a good line of reds. In the case of the albinos, it is necessary to cross the males to regular gray females and their daughters; otherwise you seem to run into a sterility problem. You can inbreed some lines for a while, but usually you have to revert to outcrossing. Most of the crosses are best accomplished with a green or red female.

To maintain a red line, once you have eliminated all of the color

impurities, it usually requires at least two, and sometimes three, separate linebred or inbred strains of reds. Even with three lines, you must be very careful in selecting your breeders; if there is any hint of black or gray in the finnage, you are in trouble. Some say it is possible to clarify the reds by outcrossing them to black or blue females. My own experiences were negative in this respect, but perhaps the females were not compatible.

Under wild conditions, a large fin development would be a hindrance for obtaining food, escaping from

quality males. While some may not agree with this statement, it can only be said that many a guppy breeder has been able to raise guppies of very high quality whereas others often have difficulties.

Breeding Methods

We have basically three different breeding methods with slightly different variations on each. They are inbreeding, linebreeding, and outcrossing.

Inbreeding

The breeding of closely related fish, such as brother to sister, father to

predators, and reproducing. But in the controlled environment of our fish rooms, we eliminate most of these factors right off the bat. However, at the same time, through the elimination of enemies and by containing the females to a small area, we also encourage breeding by inferior males. In natural conditions, breeding would only be done by the most vigorous and hardy males, thus carrying on the vitality of the species.

Most breeders feel that it is of prime importance to keep virgin-female guppies of each strain available for breeding with the best-

What to Look for in Female Guppies

Most of the really good females have a delta or wide box-shaped tail. Occasionally, good shark-tailed females will throw the best delta tails though. When working with a cross, I will usually use one of each type until it is determined which throws the best males. These will be used for future breeding.

Albino guppy strains are difficult to maintain.

76

Fancy Guppies

The Expert Knows

Breeding Age

Don't wait too long before you set up the breeders. This is probably the most common, and most preventable, mistake that is made time and time again. Of course, tank space is often the cause for delay in setting up new breeders. If you wait too long, the fish you may try to mix will be of different ages and this can cause growth problems. Additionally, females that are too old will only drop a few babies at a time and this can be frustrating to say the least.

daughter, or backcrossing the son to mother is referred to as inbreeding. The advantages of inbreeding are in fixing a fin conformation, or a particular color or color pattern. Theoretically, you would take the best male and female of a dropping and breed them to each other. Of the resulting young, you would do the same thing, and so on down through the various drops and generations. If you develop an exceptional male, you would breed him to his sister, and if possible, back to his mother and daughter. This would give you a higher percentage of closely related fish for possible development of an outstanding inbred line. This practice may be continued for a number of years with only a slight diminishing of the quality of the fish, provided care is taken in the selection of the individual breeders. Usually you will end up with fish that look alike in both pattern and color.

In most cases, a female will have several drops of young once she is impregnated by the original male. If a different male is introduced to the female and provided his sperm is viable, some of the next generation of young should be fathered by him.

This however, is not a hard-and-fast rule. Many breeders have tried to use this method, and they only mess up their lines. They assume that females taken from a mixed tank and placed with the male of their choice will result in young from this male, but if the male is sterile, they are stuck with the young from whichever male fertilized the female in the first place. Basically, it's not really a good method for controlled breeding or the maintenance of lines.

Reds are among the more challenging strains to keep pure.

Some breeders concentrate on body coloration rather than elaborate finnage.

While on the subject of inbreeding, if, for instance, you want to breed gold or albino guppies, it is usually desirable to cross a gold or albino male into a gray female. As gray is dominant over the recessive gold or albino color, all of the F_1 dropping will be gray in body color. If brother and sister are then bred together, the F_2 young will be approximately 25 percent gold and 75 percent gray (50 percent gold-gray and 25 percent gray in genetic makeup). As you are trying to establish a gold line, you would use fish for breeding that display the gold color that you are looking for. In breeding

brother and sister again with the gold-colored bodies, you should get 100 percent gold or albino, whichever the case may be. From then on, it is simply a matter of improving finnage and coloration. One of the problems encountered in working with the gold guppies is that while attempting to increase the body color, there is the tendency to lose the basic gold body coloration. To help prevent this, you would use only the males that display at least 50 percent of the basic gold body color. Even though you may not get as many body color points in the show, if you're into showing your guppies, at least such a fish wouldn't be disqualified. I raised golds for a

High quality guppies can be produced using linebreeding, but it is very important that good records be kept on the origins of the line.

number of years, taking several class championships, and mainly dropped them because of a lack of competition and the desire to use the tanks for other lines.

Linebreeding

Linebreeding is perhaps the safest and most efficient method of guppy breeding. In this, as well as in any other breeding program, it is important that good records be kept, either in your head or written down—written down is the preferred choice here. To start off a linebreeding program you would take a male and breed him to two of his sisters. The resulting young from each female would be kept separate. The F_1, or next generation would be bred again, brother to sister, keeping each line separate. You would continue this for approximately six generations. At this time, you would cross a male from one line to a female from the other line, and vice versa. These again would be kept separate. If you watch what you are doing and pick the correct fish for breeders, it is possible to continue breeding this way for years and still produce quality fish. In reality this, too, is a form of inbreeding, but by running another

Part of the fascination in raising guppies is that you have almost complete control over their environment and development.

related line to cross back into, you are able to retain many of the better qualities in fish that can be lost through a strict inbreeding program. With a little multiplication, you can see how this could get out of hand with regard to the number of tanks required to keep all these fish separate. The solution is to keep only a couple of droppings from each female. Occasionally, but only if I am using what I consider an exceptional male and female, I will keep more than two droppings.

If the time does come when you wish to try and improve on your line of inbred or linebred fish, try using a male from another good inbred or linebred line. If you use a hybrid male, you could set your breeding program back for a number of generations. With that statement we will go into the discussion of the hybrid guppy.

Outcrossing

Basically, a hybrid guppy is simply a fish or a group of fish resulting from a cross of unrelated fish. The F_1, or first generation, possesses what may

be called hybrid vigor and may be outstanding fish in size as well as color. When trying to breed these fish one to another, you more than likely will end up with junk. This is not true in all cases, but is usually what happens. Some breeders will use this method to produce their show fish, which works out fine for them while they have the two lines to make up the hybrid cross. But it sure makes it tough on the person who buys these fish hoping to end up with the same quality fish as those they purchased. This is one of the reasons why many hobbyists are reluctant to buy fish from a show unless they know the breeder and he tells the buyer if they were from a hybrid or from inbred lines. Fish from hybrid lines can be worked out with a good program of inbreeding, but it usually takes time.

Breeding Goals

At the same time, there are individuals who simply cross every fish they have in the hope of hitting the right combination and coming up with some good show fish. Once in a while it does happen, and they win big for a year or so; shortly thereafter they seem to fade away as they try to reproduce the same cross that gave them the good fish.

Don't take the above mentioned information in a way that would make you think it's unwise to obtain another line in order to improve the finnage or color of your own fish. Oftentimes this is the only way to get that extra little push your fish may need to boost them into the winner's circle.

When attempting to change the color of an existing line, it is necessary to introduce a male having the desired color to a couple of your virgin-female guppies. He would then be bred to his daughters; and if at all possible, to his granddaughters. The initial cross is unlikely to produce the color you desire, depending primarily on the compatibility of the females to the cross. By breeding him to the F_1 and F_2 females, some of the desired colored fish should crop up. Just follow your regular breeding program from there on. While the breeding of large-tailed females is not my goal, once a year a dropping or two will throw giant-tailed females. These tails are usually as large or larger than the males' and very colorful. People who see them can't believe that they have developed

While working to develop an all-black guppy, it was found that an inheritable lethal gene was involved and the fish began to die off.

naturally, but such is the case. It must be the water. They breed normally and the young are just as good as those of females with tails of normal size.

Some time ago, in trying to develop an all-black guppy, it was found that an inheritable lethal gene was involved. As the black coloration was advanced toward the head area through selective breeding, the fish began to die off. Many breeders have tried this with the same results, so it would appear that we are more or less stuck with the three-quarters or seven-eights black-bodied fish. Even if someone were able to develop an all-black fish, it would

only mean an extra point toward body color to the judges in a show, hardly a critical factor.

When working with males that have a snakeskin pattern, it is possible to use almost any virgin female and still carry the pattern into the next generation, which makes this strain one of the easiest to work with as the pattern is dominant in the males. A common weakness with this type of fish is a short or small dorsal fin.

Breeders of this type of fish seem primarily concerned only with the size of the fish, figuring perhaps this will make up for the deficiency in other areas. What many people fail to

At first glance, nearly anyone would think this is a very nice male guppy. But look at that anal fin—it's a female!

Defects

It should be common practice not to breed any fish that have discernable faults, regardless of how tempting it may be. Oftentimes, a fish may be superior in some areas but severely lacking in others. These fish should still not be used for breeding projects, as there is no way to keep the faults from continuing in the genetic makeup.

realize is that when you increase the size of a fish, the pigmentation and pattern is spread over a larger area and tends to bleach out or become dull with greater distribution. This is one of the reasons that the smaller German fish appear so brightly colored.

With some lines you can use color in the female's caudal fin as the determining factor as to which females to use for breeding. In the red lines, for example, a female with a blue cast may throw the best fish. Keep track of which ones throw the best fish for future breedings.

A great number of caudal variations have been applied to the half-black fish, often with very striking results. My work, however, has been mostly with the half-black reds. I have found it best to work with two different lines of the same strain. In most cases I will run three lines, two of the lighter bodied or gold half-black, and one of the gray-gold body. Whenever I notice one of the lines losing a little color or size, I simply cross into one of the other lines, usually with good results. A number of the breeders will use some of my fish to cross into theirs to improve the

quality of theirs. The blue females in all four of my lines seem to work out quite well when crossing for a half-black blue.

If a neutral line is not available to you, females from a light green line seem to work quite well for crossing, too. A good rule of thumb is to use fish of the same general color as those you wish to improve upon. Through selective breeding, it is sometimes possible to eliminate many characteristics. The major drawback is the amount of time invested and the number of tanks involved. Initially, in the production of the type of guppy we have today, this work was necessary. It is much easier now to obtain another line from one of the established breeders to work into your line.

Maintenance of Lines

Once a line has been developed, it now must be maintained. You'll notice that not much in the way of genetics has been presented here, which is surely fine with most people! Basically, all I have been concerned with, as far as Mendel's genetic findings apply to the guppy, are the percentages involved

Endler's livebearers have quite a few unique strains that are fun to play around with, too.

when crossing gold to gray guppies—or working with hybrids. It helps to know which colors are dominant and which are recessive, and also which body patterns are dominant. Be advised, however, that there are no hard-and-fast rules regarding pattern dominance, and there are few, if any, truly "pure" lines. While the guppy world has standards to work toward for competition, many people are quite content just to raise what they think are nice fish—and that's perfectly fine since that is all part of what makes raising guppies so enjoyable anyway.

Trying New Color Lines

Occasionally it is a good idea to try for something different. This way, it is possible to add new colors and perhaps a different pattern to your collection, but you still have your old standbys in case things don't quite go as planned. As you work with your various lines, you will find instances such as these where you are able to modify your basic colors to produce different ones.

With a four-month turnover period it is possible to develop whatever color variations you desire in a reasonable length of time, provided you pay strict

After dropping the young fish, the females generally show no interest in them.

attention to picking the right breeders and separating young males from the females. You do not want any prebred females if you are attempting to modify the color in a line.

When working with unknown lines, it might be necessary to breed a father to a couple of his daughters to fix the color. All you have to do from then on is follow the normal linebreeding practices.

Care of the Fry

Perhaps after their parentage, the most important factor in raising

quality guppies is the care they are given right after birth to the first three months of their lives. It is this period that usually makes or breaks a show-quality specimen.

It is generally a good idea to isolate the female a few days before she drops. Place her in a small tank, usually a 5-gallon (19 l) tank is good, or a drum-style bowl of some type will work, too. This serves two purposes: It prevents other fish from bothering her and also lessens the possibility of some of the babies being eaten. During their confinement, the females are fed very well with live baby brine

you can skip a feeding so that when they come to the front of the tank on your approach there is no food for them. An hour or so later, add a touch of dry food to the tank and usually they will pick at it for a few minutes. This conditions them to eating dry food, and that's when the feeding program really begins.

shrimp, frozen adult brine shrimp, and light feedings of a quality dry food. If using a drum bowl, the water is changed every other day with water taken from a healthy tank. It is advisable to place the bowls in areas where the fish will not be disturbed by your working around the tanks. You should not use fresh tap water for these bowls or for the confinement tanks; rather use only conditioned tank water so the female will feel comfortable and relaxed.

Usually a couple of days after the young are born, I transfer them to a 5- or 10-gallon (19 or 38 l) aquarium with moderate strength filtration. As soon as they have made themselves at home, they are fed lightly with baby brine shrimp. It only takes a day or so for them to get the idea that when you approach the tank they are likely to be fed.

After a day or two of feeding them all the baby brine shrimp they can eat,

Cannibalism

Cannibalism is sometimes a problem that breeders experience. Most of the time, females that eat their young are no longer used as breeders and they are offered to pet shops for inclusion in community aquariums. An exceptional female can be given a second chance, but if she behaves this way again, eliminate her from the breeding program. You won't have time to fool with fish that eat their young.

The Expert Knows
Surplus Fish

Many times local pet shops will be glad to take your surplus fish off of your hands. Usually, locally raised guppies are superior in quality to those bred by large fish farms overseas. If the fish are delayed, say due to weather problems, then the overseas guppies usually arrive in poor shape. You can trade your surplus guppies or sell them outright.

If you are planning on raising guppies just to make money, I would select a different type of fish, as guppies would need to be bred by the thousands to make a real profit. And when you add in all of the costs involved, you would be lucky to even break even. Raising guppies should be a labor of love, not a hobby geared toward lining your pockets.

Chapter 7

Beyond the

Tank

Chances are good that if you succeed with your first tank of guppies, you might become even more interested in moving on to the next stage— showing your guppies. Some long-term guppy enthusiasts never have more than a few tanks, although they occasionally upgrade to larger ones and perhaps try to produce their own strains. Most often, however, once you are bitten by the guppy bug, you start looking for places to put just a few more tanks.

History of Guppy Associations

In the United States, the American Guppy Association (AGA) was formed with Larry Konig acting as chairman. This group did a lot toward setting up some show standards. Larry also distributed a number of delta-tailed guppies to various clubs throughout the country.

After the AGA faded out of sight, a group of guppy fanciers met in Ohio to start up another organization called the Congress of Guppy Groups (COGS). The following year, the name was changed to the International Fancy Guppy Association (IFGA) which is currently still in existence. Since the inauguration of the IFGA, we have seen a great change in the development of guppy species and vast improvements in judging standards.

Profiling Hobbyists

Hobbyists can be broken down into the following groups: beginning/novice, intermediate, and advanced. Additionally, you'll have some recognized as "master breeders" and "master aquarists," of which only the master breeders are really important here since breeding guppies is covered in such detail while keeping communities of them is not.

The artistic type of hobbyist maintains several aquascaped tanks, each as beautiful as the next. Then there are pragmatic hobbyists who have tier upon tier of utilitarian tanks for breeding various species, or in this case various strains perhaps. Probably the most common type of intermediate

SMALL FRY

A Lifetime Hobby

When children get involved with tropical fish, they often become lifetime aquarists. Teens and young adults may take time off for schooling, but they usually return once they start a family.

or advanced hobbyist is the one who has several show tanks, which are often community tanks, as well as a fishroom of plainer setups for breeding and growing out fry. This is especially true when we think of guppy master breeders. Basically, anyone who has developed his or her own strain will have a selection of aquariums that are used to show off this strain, or strains in some cases, while the basement or the like is filled with more serviceable breeding units.

Even the direction that hobbyists take as they grow in the hobby can differ. Some continue to expand their hobby to include more and different fishes, which is always a good thing. Others find one or two groups of fishes that fascinate them, and they specialize in just those groups. In any case, there are several major areas into which aquarists typically expand, and probably the most common one for

Yellow delta. This is a difficult color to maintain, as they tend to change color at the show if they get too stressed during shipping.

guppy enthusiasts is in the arena of showing your prized fish.

Showing Your Guppies

Assuming that you have followed (or not followed, as the case may be) all of the methods outlined in this book, you've probably produced some pretty nice-looking fish. In many of the metropolitan areas of the country there are aquarium clubs that have shows, and you may wish to exhibit your fish at one of these shows. This is a great idea, and one that is surely worth pursuing, but you may be disappointed that such shows often encourage only mild competition and only offer a small number of classes for you to enter fish into. Thus, they may not really give you any idea of just how good your fish really are. If at all possible, I would highly recommend attending an official International Fancy Guppy Association (IFGA) show, even if it means that you must travel a distance to do so. A complete list of show

This medium blue delta is showing good dorsal color match but could use a little more body color.

events can be seen by accessing their website, www.ifga.org.

Attending an IFGA show will give you the opportunity to see some good fish as well as meet and talk to some of the guppy fanciers that make up these shows. When it comes time to judge, you may sign up as an observer and follow a judging team around and see what the judges are looking for in picking the top fish of the event. Through the efforts of a lot of dedicated individuals and hours and hours of work, we came up with a set of standards for judging the fish, running

shows, and for the judges' conduct themselves.

Becoming a Judge

In order to be a qualified as an I.F.G.A judge, you have to observe a required number of shows, and assist the judging at a required number of shows after you've passed a written examination. Then you will take a visual test, placing a group of males in the proper order using the official point system. Once you have passed all the requirements, your name is brought before the judging board for approval. Only after the successful completion of all phases of this process will you be awarded a judging card. Seminars are held at least once each year, and you are required to attend one at least every other year to retain your accreditation. The visual test is very hard to pass; many individuals who know the point system forward and backward cannot pass the visual test, and so will be unable to receive their judging card and will remain as assistant judges.

This is a shame, as some of them otherwise make excellent judges. Not everyone agrees with the rules in their entirety, but the judges follow them nevertheless. In judging, it is hard not to have a personal preference as to color, caudal fin type, or even the shape of the dorsal fin, but when judging a show, personal opinion should be set aside and judging done by adhering to the standards. At any I.F.G.A. sanctioned show, you will be virtually assured that your fish will be judged correctly and fairly.

When at all possible, try to attend the shows in person. Even if you do well, and sweep a whole class or win best of show, it is always nice to see the competition that you were up against. Of course, if you lose, then it's almost a necessity to see the winners so you'll have an idea on how to better your chances next time.

Shipping Show Fish

If you are pursuing a class championship or best of show, and are unable to bring the guppies to the event yourself, then the only way to get them there is to have them shipped via overnight or second day delivery by one of the several good quality reputable carriers in the business. If you plan on sending a large quantity of fish, then perhaps air freight is a better option. This is especially true if you live close to an airport and if the recipient of your fish has easy access to an airport on their end.

Preparing the Fish for Shipment

The preparation of your guppies for shipment is an extremely important step in the overall shipment process—especially if you expect them to do well in the show and return in good shape. Do not feed them for a minimum of 24 hours; 36 hours is even better. Take one to one and a half cups of water for each fish from their own tank. Do not add any fresh water. Always use two plastic bags, one inside the other. Some breeders invert the bags, but it is not really necessary to do so.

After adding the water and the fish, spin the bag holding the top so as to capture the air pocket, or for long shipments be sure to inject pure oxygen into the bag before spinning and sealing it with at least four rubber bands. Make sure that the bags you use are a high quality type that has a low chance of leaking. Otherwise, the chance of your fish making it alive to the show is minimal. As long as the outside of the bag is dry then the fish will likely be all right. Some people have had their guppies lost for days at

a time, and if they were packed solidly, then rarely were there any problems. It is advisable to put only one fish per bag, except when using air freight when many can be put in a single large bag.

After bagging, the fish bags should be packed into a Styrofoam container, which is then taped closed and placed into an outer cardboard shell. The outer cardboard shell is also taped closed. If they're not already marked as having live tropical fishes in them, then mark them as such, which you can easily do with either the appropriate stickers or a simple permanent marker. If you are shipping your fish outside of the United States, be sure to have any warnings written in both the language of the receiving country as well as in English.

Post-Shipping Treatment

When your fish arrive at the show site, they should be placed in conditioned water, and given the best possible care. After the show is over and hopefully with a few trophies in hand, your fish can be shipped back to you in the same way as they got there in the first place.

Guppies being packaged for shipping to a show.

A half-black red delta showing good caudal and dorsal shape.

At this point, the fish have been through a tremendous amount of stress and strain and they're generally in a weakened state. After observing the fish for several hours and provided they come to the front of the tank looking for something to eat, feed them very lightly. The next day, if everything appears normal, you can return to your regular feeding program.

When a few more days have passed, and all seems well, you can place them back into their original tank. Better safe than sorry. Even with the best of care at both ends, you can expect an approximate loss of around 10 percent of your shipped entries, so you should take this into account if you are planning on sending fish to a lot of shows. Unless they develop a disease, the fish recover very quickly and will resume their normal habits in just a few days.

Show Classes

If you are a newcomer to the show circuit, the chairperson for each show can help you determine the proper classification for your fish, advising you as to the color and fin-type classification for each group. The guppies will often change color at shows, so what you had as a nice green at home might end up being disqualified because it appears blue at the show. Usually at the shows they

A pleasing light purple male. However, darker colored specimens generally do better at shows.

will list the type of lighting to be used so you can tell the true color of your fish and then enter them into the proper categories accordingly.

In the male classes, you may add a female if you choose; she will not be judged. Some exhibitors feel that the female will get the male to display better, but after some time without food, the females often nip at the male's tail and thus you are left with a male that now has no chance of winning anything at all for that show.

Often, fish that were very dark in your tanks will brighten up when placed in the show container. As a rule, fish that are very light in color are left home, unless their color is very intense. Also, those that are active seem to attract the attention of judges more so than those that are lazy or inactive. Judges are not allowed to place anything in the containers to move the fish around, so they can only judge what they can see. A reasonable effort is made to get them up and swimming, but if they fail to do so, you can pretty much forget about them placing in the show.

If you are attempting to modify a particular color, take some of these fish to a show

Beyond the Tank

and see how they compare to others in their category. If they win that's fine, but the real goal is to see how stiff the competition may be in the future. You will maintain somewhat of a narrow view of your fish unless you are able to compare them to others that are out there.

In entering the matched male classes, for some reason an important factor is that the bodies are supposed to be all the same size. Sometimes, many of us think too much emphasis placed on this. Basically what you do is judge one fish and point him on all three areas and compare the others to him. For instance, the color match on the dorsal and caudal fins should be the same; body color, body color patches or dots should also be the

same. If there are any color variations in the caudal, or in the form of different shades or patterns, it should be the same in all the fish. The size of caudal fin along with its shape is very important and all the fish presented should be equal.

The same should hold true for the dorsal fins. Another very useful trick, if you plan to enter the breeder class which consists of submitting five matched males for judging, is to bring seven or eight of them to the show. After they have settled in and colored up, then pick the five best while there. Normally, in the two matched male class you are able to color match them at home and they should still be very close after transporting them to the show.

This is a half black red female of excellent quality.

The classes that continuously present the most problems are the blue, green, and purple classes. Lighting is such an important factor in bringing out the proper color that these three classes are generally placed in an area of the show where you have some frontal light. Front sunlight would be ideal, but this is impossible to have at most of the shows. Hand-held lights of various designs have been tried, but depending on the angle they were held, as well as the angle the fish were viewed from, you could perceive three different colors in one fish. Most of the shows will use overhead fluorescent lighting placed above and between the show racks—not perfect, but they do a fair job.

Always try to enter your fish a few hours before the judging is set to begin. Doing so allows your fish to calm down a little and let their colors come out. During the actual judging there is quite a bit of moving the jars around, and if the fish has just been entered in the class, his color may not be what it should be. Your water should be as clear as possible in the show container; if colored too much, the entry could be disqualified. Also, the judges prefer to look through nice, clear water. Minor points, perhaps, but it could mean an extra point or so for your fish. As is so often the case, one point can make

This eight month old took best of show. Note the exceptional caudal.

the difference between placing and not placing.

As in any competition, it is to your benefit if you know what the judges are looking for. If you are unable to attend a show, you can request a qualified judge to check your fish after the competition is over and note areas where your entry could have been improved.

Bragging Rights

Even though my fish have won hundreds of awards, I think my biggest thrill came at a major New York City show where my blues took all twelve places in the class along with best of show single, best of show matched males, and first prize breeder male.

Glossary: Guppies

albino: a guppy with no melanin (dark pigment) in the body. Such a fish has a pinkish white body and red eyes. It may show red pigmentation, as well as blue iridescence, which is due to refraction of blue light rather than a blue pigment. The fins may be red or blue.

all-red: a guppy strain in which the male has red color throughout the body, as opposed to a "red guppy," which just has a red tail.

AOC: a miscellaneous category at guppy shows. For "all other colors."

bicolor: a guppy strain in which the male has two colors in the tail.

breeding trap: a device in which a pregnant female guppy is contained, which floats in an aquarium. Slots or perforations enable newborn fry to exit the trap and get away from their mother's predation.

bronze: a golden body color marked by dark edges on the scales.

cobra: a variety of snakeskin in which the caudal peduncle has vertical barring.

Endler's: Endler's guppy or Endler's livebearer is a close guppy relative that has become very popular. It is quite likely the fish that has recently been described as *Poecilia wingei*.

fancy guppy: any of the domesticated strains of guppies, as opposed to wild or Trinidad guppies.

gold: a body color of golden yellow.

gonopodium: the modified anal fin of a male poeciliid (e.g., guppy) that serves as an intromittent organ to place sperm into the vent of the female.

grass/glass guppy: a guppy strain marked by a caudal fin with many black spots.

gravid: carrying fry, pregnant.

gravid spot: a dark, roughly triangular spot on the belly of a female guppy. It grows and darkens during gestation.

gestation period: the time during which the female carries the developing fry, about a month for guppies, though shorter at higher temperatures and longer at lower ones.

gray: a gray body color, the wild-type color.

half black: any strain of guppy in which the rear half of the body is black in both sexes. Also tuxedo.

IFGA: the International Fancy Guppy Association, www.ifga.org.

Lebistes: the original genus in which guppies were described as *Lebistes reticulata*. They are now known as *Poecilia reticulata*, but there is some talk of resurrecting the genus in a revamping of the genus *Poecilia*.

Moscow guppy: originally an Eastern European strain showing a blue head, there are Moscows with a single body and fin color in blue, green, and purple.

multi: or multicolor. A guppy strain in which the male has three or more colors in the tail.

pastel: a guppy strain in which the male has light or white color in the finnage.

roundtail: a guppy strain in which the male has a round tail with no points.

solid: a guppy strain in which the male has a tail of a solid single color.

snakeskin: a guppy strain that has a snakeskin appearance, known as an "uninterrupted chain link" pattern on the body and perhaps on the fins.

swordtail: a guppy strain in which the male has an extension of rays in the caudal fin. This can be single (either top or bottom sword) or double (swords on both top and bottom of the tail). Only the sword is colored; the rest of the tail is clear.

Trinidad guppy: a guppy that resembles the original wild-caught fish, without the elaborate finnage and colors of selectively bred strains of fancy guppies and named for the location from which the fish originated. These are most commonly seen as "feeder guppies." Also wild guppy.

tuxedo: any strain of guppy in which the rear half of the body is black in both sexes. Also half black.

variegated: bicolor or multi, having more than one color in the tail, as opposed to solid.

virgin female: an unmated female. Since guppies can be impregnated at a very young age, and since they store sperm for many months to fertilize successive batches of young, obtaining virgin females is vital to most breeding programs. This requires daily observation and separation of growing fry.

wild guppy: a guppy that resembles the original wild-caught fish, without the elaborate finnage and colors of selectively bred strains of fancy guppies. Also Trinidad guppy, referring to the location from which the fish originated.

Dorsal Fin

Caudal Fin

Gonopodium

Glossary: General Aquarium

acid water: water with more hydrogen ions than hydroxyl ions, i.e., water with a pH below 7.0.

adipose fin: a small fleshy fin without spines behind the dorsal and present on some fishes.

aeration: agitation or other water movement that facilitates the inputting of oxygen and removal of carbon dioxide from aquarium water. Both air and water pumps can be used to aerate an aquarium. It is the movement of the water, not the air bubbles, that accomplishes the aeration. See **gas exchange**, **oxygenation**.

aerobic: occurring in the presence of oxygen.

airstone: a porous device, often ceramic but sometimes of wood, that releases a stream of air bubbles into the aquarium when attached to an air pump.

algae: this non-technical term refers to a wide variety of photosynthetic organisms, both prokaryotes and eukaryotes, including single-celled creatures like cyanobacteria, diatoms, and dinoflagellates as well as multicellular red, brown, and green seaweeds such as kelp. "Algae" is plural; the singular is "alga."

alkalinity: the buffering capacity of water that resists acidification, depending mostly on dissolved carbonates and bicarbonates. Water with low alkalinity can experience rapid and dangerous drops in pH.

Sometimes misleadingly called "carbonate hardness."

anal fin: the single fin posterior to the fish's vent. See the **ventral fin**.

anerobic: occurring in the absence of oxygen.

anoxic: occurring in the presence of extremely low levels of oxygen.

aquarium: technically any container used to hold water for keeping fish, but usually made of five panels of glass in a rectangular prism.

basic water: water with more hydroxyl ions than hydrogen ions, i.e., water with a pH above 7.0.

BBS: acronym for baby brine shrimp.

biofiltration: the use of bacterial colonies to remove toxic ammonia and nitrite from aquarium water. A biofilter must be carefully nurtured when an aquarium is first set up. See **cycling**.

blackworms: small aquatic worms widely used as live food for aquarium fish.

brackish: water with measurable salinity, but less salty than seawater; occurs naturally wherever freshwater rivers meet the ocean.

brine shrimp: crustaceans of the genus *Artemia* that live in hypersaline habitats. An extremely popular fish food, used live, frozen, and freeze-dried.

canister filter: an aquarium filter that houses media in a canister through which aquarium water is pumped under pressure. This is an extremely efficient filtration method, ideal for large aquaria.

carnivore: a fish whose diet consists primarily of animal material.

caudal fin: the tail fin of a fish.

caudal peduncle: the muscular end of a fish's body to which the tail fin attaches, typically narrower than the rest of the body.

chemical filtration: removing dissolved pollutants from aquarium water, usually by adsorption into a bed of activated carbon.

crossbreed: to mate fish of one strain with those of another. This is done either to strengthen an inbred strain or to bring in desired traits that are lacking in the strain but present in the other. See **outcross**.

cycling: establishing the biofilter in a new aquarium. The process involves allowing ammonia to build up to feed nitrifying bacterial colonies, followed by allowing nitrite to build up to feed other colonies, and ending with a mature biofilter.

Daphnia: a genus of freshwater crustaceans that are widely used a food for aquarium fishes. Also known as "water fleas."

delta tail: the ideal delta tail is a perfect triangle, like the Greek letter .

denitrification: the anaerobic process in which bacteria convert nitrate to nitrogen gas.

dorsal fin: a fin on a fish's back. Almost all fish have a dorsal fin, some types of fish have two dorsal fins, and a few primitive species have numerous dorsals.

eye spot: a "fake eye" marking of a fish's body or fin, thought to confuse predators into targeting less vital body parts. See **ocellus**.

filter feeder: a fish that feeds by straining water through its gills, retaining any small plants or animals and releasing the water. See **planktonivore**.

filtration: cleansing of aquarium water. See **mechanical filtration**, **chemical filtration**, and **biofiltration**.

fry: baby fish, singular or plural: "one fry" or "many fry."

gas exchange: the inputting of oxygen and removal of carbon dioxide from aquarium water through agitation or other water movement. Both air and water pumps can be used to move the water to facilitate gas exchange. See **aeration**, **oxygenation**.

gills: a fish's organs of respiration, consisting of finely branched, capillary-rich tissue. Breathing forces water over the gills, in the mouth and out the **opercula**. Gas exchange takes place in and some wastes are secreted by the gills.

hard water: water with a high concentration of dissolved minerals, principally calcium and magnesium.

head-and-lateral-line erosion (HLLE): a deterioration of the sensory pits on a fish's head and flanks, which can cause severe damage if untreated. There are several postulated causes, including infection, dietary deficiencies, and poor water quality.

herbivore: a fish whose diet consists primarily of plant material.

hybrid: in a strict sense, an organism whose parents were of different species; sometimes incorrectly used to refer to crossbred animals. Several popular aquarium fish are of hybrid origin, especially livebearers.

ich: sometimes "ick." Whitespot disease, a parasitic infection by the ciliated protozoan *Ichthyophthirius multifiliis*, that encysts on a fish's skin and gills. Potentially lethal, but treatable with salt, heat, chemicals, or a combination of these.

inbreed: to make use of any breeding program that mates close relatives such as father-daughter or brother-sister. It is very useful for fixing traits but in excess it can lead to weak fish and genetic abnormalities.

Infusoria: a term for a multitude of microscopic organisms widely used to feed fry too small to consume BBS.

interspecific: between individuals of different species (e.g., interspecific aggression).

intraspecific: between members of one species (e.g., intraspecific aggression).

labyrinth fish: an anabantoid fish possessing a labyrinth organ, a structure used to extract oxygen from atmospheric air much like a lung.

lateral line: a row of pit-like sensory organs along the side of a fish's body.

linebreed: to breed related fish while avoiding the excesses of strict inbreeding, usually by mating less closely related fish. Often several familial lines of a strain are maintained and occasionally outcrossed to each other.

livebearer: technically any fish that gives birth to live young as opposed to laying eggs, but most commonly referring to the family Poeciliidae.

mechanical filtration: removing suspended debris from aquarium water, usually by passing it through pads of various fibers or foam.

micropredator: a fish that feeds on small organisms like worms and crustaceans.

microworms: non parasitic nematodes that are grown in a cereal-based medium as fish food. Widely used as a substitute or complement for BBS.

mouthbrooding: a reproductive strategy in which the eggs are incubated in a parent fish's throat. After release, the fry may be taken back into the mouth when threatened.

nauplius (pl. nauplii): the free-swimming larval stage of many crustaceans, such as brine shrimp.

nitrification: the aerobic process in which bacteria convert ammonia into nitrite, and then nitrite to nitrate.

ocellus (pl. ocelli): a "fake eye" marking of a fish's body or fin, thought to confuse predators into lunging for less vital body parts. See **eye spot**.

omnivore: a fish whose diet consists of both plant and animal material.

operculum (pl. opercula): a fish's gill cover. Many fish flare these out perpendicular to their body as part of a threat or courting display.

outcross: to mate fish of one strain with those of another. This is done either to strengthen an inbred strain or to bring in desired traits that are lacking in the strain but present in the other. See **crossbreed**.

oviparous: reproduction in which the eggs are laid or scattered, then undergo incubation in the aquatic environment. See **ovoviviparous** and **viviparous**.

ovoviviparous: reproduction in which the eggs are retained within the female's body until they hatch, at which time the fry are born. The female, however, does not provide nourishment beyond the egg. See **oviparous** and **viviparous**.

oxygenation: the dissolving of oxygen into water, also by implication the removal of dissolved carbon dioxide from the water. See **gas exchange**.

paired fins: the fins of a fish that come in pairs, one on each side of the body. These include the **pectoral** and **pelvic fins**.

parasite: an organism that depends on the presence of another organism to carry out life functions for it. A parasite usually lives within the body tissues of its host. Many fish diseases are caused by parasites.

pectoral fins: the fins behind the operculum, similar to our arms.

pelvic fins: the fins in front of the anus, similar to our legs.

pH: a logarithmic measurement of how acid or basic water is, for *pondus hydrogeni*. The usual range is 0 to 14, with 7 being defined as neutral. Most fish do well with a pH of between 6 and 8.

pigment: substances which produce a fish's color. A pigment can be either a substance of a particular color or a clear crystal which refracts light to reflect a certain color. Fish often have both types of pigments.

piscivore: a fish whose diet consists primarily of other fishes.

planktonivore: a fish whose diet consists primarily tiny organisms (plankton). See **filter feeder**.

powerhead: a small submersible water pump.

predator: a fish that feeds on other animals.

prey: a fish that is eaten by another animal.

reverse osmosis (RO): a process which uses water pressure to force water through a membrane, leaving most dissolved substances behind. This produces extremely pure water with no hardness or alkalinity; such water is used to mix artificial seawater and as a major component in water mixes for fish that require very soft, very acid environments.

secondary sex characteristics: gender-linked physical traits not part of the reproductive organs, such as sex-dependent coloration or finnage.

soft water: water with a low concentration of dissolved minerals.

substrate: the material on the bottom of an aquarium, typically sand or gravel, but sometimes mud, peat, or other substances.

swim bladder: an sac-like organ in most fishes that is inflated with air or with other gases and that the fish uses to modify its buoyancy in order to move upward or downward in the water. Diseases of the swim bladder manifest in an inability to maintain proper buoyancy—usually with the fish floating helplessly at the surface.

top off: to add water to an aquarium to make up for water lost through evaporation.

undergravel filter (UGF): a filter that uses the gravel bed of the aquarium as its medium. A slotted plate sits under the gravel, with lift tubes through which an airstone or a powerhead draws water down through the gravel bed and up from under the plate. A **reverse-flow UGF** uses a powerhead to pump water down the tubes, under the plate, and up through the gravel bed.

unpaired fins: the fins of a fish that are single and insert into the mid-sagittal plane. These include the **caudal**, **dorsal**, and **ventral fins**.

veiltail: a fish with a tail greatly enlarged compared to the wild type. Usually the other fins are also elongated.

velvet: a parasitic infection by a dinoflagellate in the genus *Oodinium*. The spots are much smaller than with ich and may be yellowish. This is also a potentially lethal and highly contagious disease, but also treatable with salt, heat, chemicals, or a combination of these.

ventral fin: the single fin posterior to the fish's vent. Also the **anal fin**.

viviparous: reproduction in which the eggs are retained within the female, and the developing young are nourished in some way from the female's body until they are born. See **oviparous** and **ovoviviparous**.

water change: the removal of a volume of water from an aquarium and its replacement with the same volume of clean, fresh water, performed to remove wastes from the aquarium. Water changes are a simple and effective maintenance procedure for all aquaria and should be large and frequent.

Resources

Magazines

Tropical Fish Hobbyist
1 T.F.H. Plaza
3rd & Union Avenues
Neptune City, NJ 07753
Phone: (732) 988-8400
E-mail: info@tfh.com
www.tfhmagazine.com

Internet Resources

A World of Fish
www.aworldoffish.com

Aquarium Hobbyist
www.aquariumhobbyist.com

FINS: The Fish Information Service
http://fins.actwin.com

Fish Geeks
www.fishgeeks.com

Fish Index
www.fishindex.com

MyFishTank.Net
www.myfishtank.net

Water Wolves
http://forums.waterwolves.com

Associations & Societies

Association of Aquarists
David Davis, Membership Secretary
2 Telephone Road
Portsmouth, Hants, England
PO4 0AY
Phone: 01705 798686

British Killifish Association
Adrian Burge, Publicity Officer
E-mail: adjan@wym.u-net.com
www.bka.org.uk

**Canadian Association of
Aquarium Clubs**
Miecia Burden, Membership
Coordinator
142 Stonehenge Pl.
Kitchener, Ontario, Canada
N2N 2M7
Phone: (517) 745-1452
E-mail: mbburden@look.ca
www.caoac.on.ca

**Federation of American Aquarium
Societies**
Jane Benes, Secretary
923 Wadsworth Street
Syracuse, NY 13208-2419
Phone: (513) 894-7289
E-mail: jbenes01@yahoo.com
www.gcca.net/faas

**International Fancy Guppy
Association**
Rick Grigsby, Secretary
3552 West Lily Garden Lane
South Jordan, Utah 84095
Phone: (801) 694-7425
E-mail: genx632@yahoo.com
www.ifga.org

National Aquarium in Baltimore
501 E. Pratt Street
Baltimore, Maryland 21202.
Phone: (410) 576-3800
www.aqua.org

Resources

Index

Index

(note: numbers in boldface denote captions)

About the Author

Stan Shubel started raising guppies in the 1940s. Since then, he has been responsible for many of the initial high-quality guppies that have formed as the base by the worlds top guppy breeders to build upon. With hundreds of awards to his name, Stan is widely considered one of the world's leading authorities on fancy guppies.

Photo Credits

Photos courtesy of TFH archives and Stan Shubel

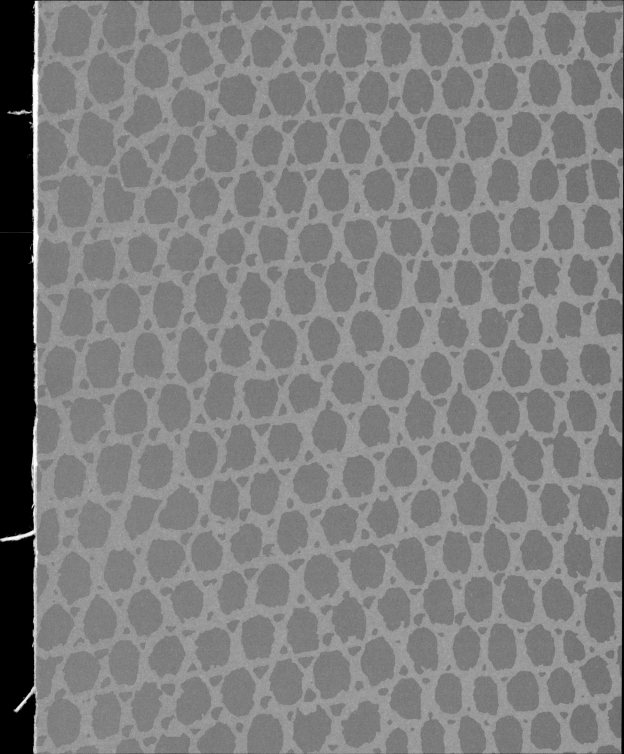

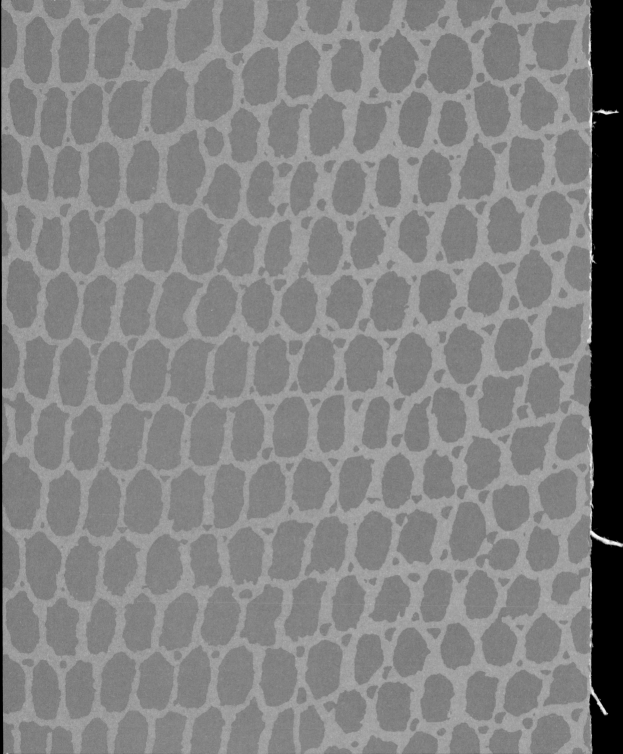